Freedom of Choice in Education

**THE MACMILLAN COMPANY**
NEW YORK · CHICAGO
DALLAS · ATLANTA · SAN FRANCISCO
LONDON · MANILA
IN CANADA
**BRETT-MACMILLAN LTD.**
GALT, ONTARIO

# FREEDOM OF CHOICE IN EDUCATION

Virgil C. Blum, S.J.

*The Macmillan Company*
*New York · 1958*

Imprimi Potest    Leo J. Burns, S.J.

Milwaukee, Wis.
April 2, 1958


Nihil Obstat     John A. Schulien
                 Censor Librorum
Milwaukee, Wis.
July 5, 1958


Imprimatur      ✠ Albertus G. Meyer
                 Archiepiscopus Milwauchiensis
Milwauchiae
die 16a iulii 1958

The *nihil obstat* and *imprimatur* are official declarations that a book is free of doctrinal or moral error. No implication is contained therein that those who have granted the *nihil obstat* and *imprimatur* agree with the contents, opinions, or statements expressed.

First Printing

Library of Congress catalog card number: 58-11540

The Macmillan Company, New York
Brett-Macmillan Ltd., Galt, Ontario

Printed in the United States of America

# Acknowledgment

Grateful acknowledgment is hereby made to the following publishers and authors for use of copyrighted materials: from THE WEB OF GOVERNMENT by R. M. MacIver, copyright 1949, The Macmillan Company, New York; from ADVENTURES OF IDEAS by Alfred North Whitehead, copyright 1933, The Macmillan Company, New York; from ON LIBERTY . . . by John Stuart Mill, copyright 1926, The Macmillan Company, New York; from THE PROTESTANT CRUSADE by Ray Allen Billington, copyright 1938, The Macmillan Company, New York; from HORACE MANN AND RELIGION IN THE MASSACHUSETTS PUBLIC SCHOOLS by Raymond B. Culver, copyright 1929, Yale University Press, New Haven; from CRISIS IN EDUCATION by Bernard Iddings Bell, copyright 1949 by Bernard Iddings Bell, McGraw-Hill Book Co., Inc., New York; from "The Road to Totalitarianism" by Henry Hazlitt, an essay in ON FREEDOM AND FREE ENTERPRISE, edited by Mary Sennholz, copyright 1956, D. Van Nostrand Company, Inc., Princeton, N.J.; from THE UNIVERSITIES OF EUROPE IN THE MIDDLE AGES by Hastings Rashdall, copyright 1936, Clarendon Press, Oxford, England; from REFLECTIONS ON GOVERNMENT by Ernest Barker, copyright 1951, Oxford University Press, New York; from DOCUMENTS OF AMERICAN HISTORY, edited by Henry Steele Commager, copyright 1949, Appleton-Century-Crofts, Inc., New York; from "The Role of Government in Education" by Milton Friedman, an essay in ECONOMICS AND THE PUBLIC INTEREST, edited by Robert A. Solo, copyright 1955, Rutgers University Press, New Brunswick, N.J.; from GREAT POLITICAL THINKERS by William Ebenstein, copyright second edition 1956, Rinehart & Company, New York; from HE WHO IS: A STUDY IN TRADITIONAL THEISM by E. L. Mascall, copyright 1943, Longmans, Green and Co., New York; from THE RE-

LATION OF THE STATE TO RELIGIOUS EDUCATION IN MASSACHU-
SETTS by Sherman M. Smith, copyright 1926, Syracuse Uni-
versity Book Store, Syracuse, N.Y.; from FREEDOM IN CON-
TEMPORARY SOCIETY by Samuel Eliot Morison, copyright 1956,
Little, Brown and Company and Atlantic Monthly Press,
Boston, Mass.; from NOTES ON THE STATE OF VIRGINIA by
Thomas Jefferson, edited by William Peden, copyright 1955,
The University of North Carolina Press, Chapel Hill, N.C.;
from EDUCATION OF THE FOUNDING FATHERS OF THE REPUBLIC
by James J. Walsh, copyright 1935, Fordham University
Press, New York; from AMERICAN INTERPRETATIONS OF NA-
TURAL LAW by Benjamin Wright, copyright 1931, Harvard
University Press, Cambridge, Mass.; from PRINCIPLES OF SO-
CIAL AND POLITICAL THEORY by Ernest Barker, copyright 1951,
Clarendon Press, Oxford, England; from ORIGINS OF AMERICAN
SCIENTISTS, by R. H. Knapp and B. H. Goodrich, copyright
1952, The University of Chicago Press, Chicago; from GOD IN
EDUCATION by Henry Pitney Van Dusen, copyright 1951,
Charles Scribner's Sons, New York; from THE REPORT OF THE
COMMISSION ON FINANCING HIGHER EDUCATION: Nature and
Needs of Higher Education, copyright 1951, Columbia Uni-
versity Press, N.Y.; from "Implications of Increasing Enroll-
ments for Academic Standards and Methods" by Martin
Quanbeck, *The Educational Record*, XXXVIII (April, 1957);
from "Administrative Ethics and the Rule of Law" by F.
Morstein Marx, *American Political Science Review*, XLIII
(Dec., 1949); from "Educational News and Editorial Com-
ment" by Procter Thomson, *The School Review*, LXIII
(April, 1955); from "The Freedom to Believe" by Wilber G.
Katz, *The Atlantic Monthly*, Vol. 192 (October, 1953); from
"The Black Silence of Fear" by The Honorable William O.
Douglas, *The New York Times Magazine*, January 13, 1952;
from "Invasions of the First Amendment Through Condi-

tioned Public Spending" by Alanson W. Willcox, Vol. 41, *Cornell Law Quarterly* (Fall, 1955); from "The Fifth Freedom" by Seymour St. John, *The Saturday Review*, XXXVI (October 10, 1953); from "The Sectarian Conflict Over Church and State" by Will Herberg, *Commentary*, XIV (Nov., 1952); from "Liberty, the State, and the School" by George K. Gardner, *Law and Contemporary Problems*, XX (Winter, 1955); from "Know How vs. Know Why" by Bernard Iddings Bell, *Life* (October 11, 1950); from "Will Scholarships Give U.S. Better-Trained Scientists" by M. M. Boring (A Copyrighted Interview), *U.S. News & World Report*, XLIV (Jan. 24, 1958); from Address Before the Los Angeles Chamber of Commerce, June 22, 1956, by Arnold O. Beckman; and from "We are Less Educated than 50 Years Ago" by Arthur Bestor (A Copyrighted Interview), *U.S. News & World Report*, XLI (Nov. 30, 1956).

To the Memory of
The Lords Baltimore of Maryland
who brought religious
liberty to America

# Foreword

Pluralism is the mark of every open society. American society has its pluralistic diversity built into its institutions at every level of life. In economics, in politics, in culture, we are proud of our pluralism, and of the corresponding freedom it assures. There is one field, however, in which pluralism seems to arouse the suspicion, even the resentment, of a considerable number of liberal Americans, and that is the field of education. In education, especially in education at the lower levels, many Americans otherwise committed to diversity seem to feel that uniformity is mandatory, and that pluralism is "divisive" and "undemocratic." In this area, government monopoly, otherwise so repugnant to the American genius, is felt to be right and proper, for it is held to be the "natural" function of the government to educate the rising generation so as to assure the unity and solidarity of the nation. Nongovernmental education must, of course, be tolerated; but because of the threat to democracy alleged to be inherent in it, it is to be denied public support beyond the bare legal recognition guaranteed by the Supreme Court in the celebrated Oregon decision.

There are many reasons for this puzzling anomaly in the American liberal consciousness, and many explanations that are put to use as rationalizations in the liberal mind. It does not seem to be realized, however, that such an attitude is, in fact, profoundly illiberal since it not only discourages pluralism and diversity in a crucial area of our culture, but also substantially denies freedom of choice in a field where, above all, freedom of choice would seem to be desirable and necessary. Parents may, indeed, set up their own schools for their children, or delegate the responsibility for doing so to their church, and if these schools meet the standard requirements set for public education they are entitled to full recognition

xi

under the law. But parents who choose to take advantage of their right are heavily penalized, since under present practices they can receive only minimal aid from the community, and this despite the fact that in providing educational facilities these schools are obviously performing a public service of the first order. Instead of welcoming nongovernmental schools, when properly accredited, as a valuable element in the cultural diversity we all profess to desire, we tend rather to frown upon them as somehow a threat to our way of life, and to refuse them the full and open recognition that they would seem to deserve in view of the service they render and the basic parental rights they are designed to implement. In every area of life, freedom of choice and voluntary nongovernmental activity are encouraged as profoundly in harmony with the American pluralistic ethos; here alone they are disapproved of and penalized as an invasion of an essential governmental monopoly. We are pluralists everywhere else, but somehow we remain statists and uniformitarians in the realm of education.

Americans are becoming increasingly uneasy about this gross discrepancy in their democratic philosophy, and they are groping for some way of promoting diversity and freedom of choice in education. Since most of the nongovernmental schools in this country are schools under church or religious auspices, the problem, difficult enough on its own account, is further bedeviled by the emotion-charged issue that goes under the rubric of the "separation of church and state." Contrary to the facts of history, contrary to the continuing mind of the American people, contrary to the general burden of Supreme Court decisions, it is still vehemently asserted in certain quarters that due recognition of the independent school as a public educational institution performing a public educational function would be a violation of the establishment-of-religion clause in the First Amendment to the Federal Constitution. Any plan for encouraging pluralism and freedom of choice in education can hardly afford to ignore this side of the problem.

Virgil C. Blum's "tax credit" plan, presented in detail in this book, would seem to take all of these considerations into account. Father Blum is keenly aware of the strange anomaly presented by a uniformitarian educational philosophy embedded in the pluralistic ethos of American democracy. He is keenly aware of the gross injustice involved in penalizing parents for exercising their freedom of choice in education, even to the limited degree it is possible to do so today. He is keenly aware, too, of the larger issues involved, for he well understands that in a real sense education is not simply one of the many activities of a society, but that activity in which the very inwardness of the society is revealed, almost as much as in its religion. In the "tax credit" plan, Father Blum seems to have developed a way of dealing with the problem that does justice to its many complexities and is calculated to appeal to the thinking of large groups of Americans. It is a moderate, reasonable, and practical program, carefully conceived and carefully worked out, concerned alike with the public school and with the independent school, but concerned most of all with the future of freedom and education in this country. I myself, who have been preoccupied with the problem of American education for many years, have profited greatly from a study of Father Blum's work; and though I might want to make qualifications here and there, of one kind or another, I feel myself greatly indebted to him for what he is doing to bring the whole question, in all its urgency, to the attention of the American people.

August 1958                                WILL HERBERG

# Contents

Freedom of Choice in Education

# I

# Freedom of Choice
# in Education

The USSR challenge to world freedom is a challenge to America to solve its educational problems. Our freedom and the freedom of all men may hinge on how we meet the challenge. If we are to counter the challenge of a powerful scientific totalitarian state vowed to our destruction, we must develop the intellectual capacities of our children and youth to their highest potential. But in our efforts to achieve this important objective, we must cling tenaciously to the principles of freedom and democracy.

It will not be easy to remedy our educational deficiencies. But in our determination to do so, we must adopt methods that safeguard the freedom of the human mind and spirit. This is only to say that our educational policy must be philosophically based on the dignity and transcendent value of the individual, on the integrity and freedom of the human person; it must be legally based on the Federal Constitution, recognizing the individual student clothed in all his constitutional rights. While the Soviet educational system is based on enforced conformity to Communist doctrines, our educational system must be based, if we are to remain a free and democratic people, on the principle of freedom of choice in education.

A free society recognizes the paramount importance of the individual person who bears the image of God. This is of the essence of constitutional government. It is limited government. It is government limited by the inalienable God-given rights of the person. In promoting the common good and discharging its functions, limited government gives full recognition to the inalienable and constitutional rights of the individual.

Here lies the essential difference between a free society and an enslaved society. In a free society the individual has paramount importance. In an enslaved society the individual is just a cog in a vast power-driven machine. In a free society the individual, marked by his transcendent worth and clothed in his constitutional rights, is the measure of what the state may do. In an enslaved society the individual, degraded to the level of a material entity and stripped of all his personal rights, is a mere tool for what the state wills to do.

In such a society the individual has no recognizable rights against the state; he is forced to conform to the state's thought and will. He is a unit in a system—a system that submerges the individual into a uniform mass to the complete loss of his individuality and identity.

It should be apparent that freedom is more than the negative right not to be forced to conform. It is a positive right. And there exists in the state the corresponding positive duty to provide the conditions necessary for the exercise of freedom. Hence a free society must perform two positive functions respecting the freedoms of its citizens. First, it must protect the rights and liberties of the individual person. Second, it must provide the conditions, within recognized limitations, that enable the individual to develop his own personality consistently with his own fundamental beliefs and convictions. A society that denies to the individual the conditions of freedom and forces him, against his convictions and beliefs, to conform to a particular philosophical and theological orientation violates the basic principles of freedom.

A government dedicated to the preservation of freedom dispenses its services and discharges its functions consistent with the rights of individuals. It will not force a citizen to surrender his constitutional rights as a condition for sharing in public benefits. It will protect his rights while rendering services to him. The functions of government, says the English political scientist Ernest Barker, "are always, in their nature, functions of service rendered to rights and therefore rendered to persons, *individual* persons, who own these rights as the necessary conditions of the development in action of their individual personality." [1] In a free society the individual person, clothed in all his constitutional rights, must occupy the center of the stage. Regardless of the number and variety of welfare services and functions a state may provide, they are always "rendered to rights" and therefore "to individual persons" who possess these rights as "the necessary conditions" for achieving their personal development.

The centrality of the individual, however, is today being challenged. With the growth of government functions and services, to what extent can individual persons retain their individuality? In other words, to what extent will government force the individual to conform to a mass pattern? The complete submersion of the individual into the mass state—this is the danger of the welfare state. This is a danger that threatens the freedom of the individual and of society. The individual person, once free and self-determining, is in danger of being progressively more and more caught up into the orbit of government control and regulation through the imposition of restrictive controls as the condition for sharing in the benefits of welfare legislation. When this happens, the individual loses more and more of his autonomy; the government makes more and more of his decisions; it does more and more of his thinking. This develops the mass man; group thinking prevails. Individual personality is destroyed.

The increasing extension of state power seems inevitable. But freedom demands the preservation of islands of independence beyond the reach of direct government control. These are the islands that must be held in the face of increasing state power. They are voluntary associations organized by free individuals to carry on particular activities within the broad confines of a free society. Such associations are not part of the state, but are part of the nonlegal community called society. The state is "the community permanently organized in a single legal association, for the one legal purpose of declaring and enforcing universal and uniform rules. . . ." Society, on the other hand, is "the community organized . . . in a number of voluntary associations for a variety of purposes . . . which adorn and supplement . . . the activity proper to the purpose of the legal organization." [2]

A free society supposes the freedom of individuals to organize voluntary associations for specific purposes. The purpose of particular associations is to carry on activities and to perform functions that promote the objectives of the members in a manner consistent with the general welfare. Such associations may be as varied as the objectives for which individuals may combine their efforts. These objectives may be completely beyond the reach of individuals, but within the easy reach of individuals organized into groups. They may be religious, cultural, charitable, educational, professional, economic, occupational, social, and others.

Voluntary associations have their origin in the thought and aspirations of free individuals. They are incubated in a society characterized by diversity of thought, a society that allows its members a wide range in the pursuit of truth. Freedom of thought and belief is the essential condition for the organization of voluntary associations and for the conduct of their particular activities. Government thought control means government control, at least indirectly, of all associations.

Consequently, the best bulwark against government control of voluntary associations is freedom of choice in education. This is the freedom to attend any approved school or college without being deprived of equal state educational benefits. This gives rise to an important question. Can voluntary associations survive if government deprives its citizens of freedom of choice in education and thus impairs that freedom and diversity of thought essential for free group action?

When government demands the surrender of freedom of choice in education as a condition for sharing in state educational benefits, it enforces conformity to the philosophical and theological orientation of government schools. Under such conditions of coercive conformity, can that freedom and diversity of thought essential to the establishment and conduct of voluntary associations endure?

The extension of state power is inversely proportionate to the number and autonomy of voluntary associations. If a large share of individual and group objectives are not achieved through voluntary action, they will be secured by the uniform and compulsory action of the state, with a necessary increase in the exercise of government power. The greater the activities of voluntary associations, the greater the freedom of the individual; the greater the scope of compulsory state regulations, the less the freedom of the individual.[3]

For the preservation of freedom of action, it is imperative that, although state action is necessary in an organized legal community, we strive to achieve through voluntary action all those ends and objectives of organized society which are not of their nature functions of government. "We do our best if we do what we can for ourselves, by voluntary social co-operation, before we invoke the action of the State . . . ," remarked Professor Barker.[4]

Thus, the use of voluntary associations is based on the proposition that to achieve a particular objective free action is preferable to coerced action. "It is a conclusion in favour of the maximum of voluntary self-help by groups of individuals, voluntarily acting for themselves in the social area; thinking out for themselves, in their own sphere of interest, the requirements and conditions of their own development; and, when they have thought them out *for* themselves, going on to achieve them *by* themselves, and by their own efforts, so far as in their own sphere they can." [5]

The existence of voluntary associations is an important condition of liberty. One of the major conditions that make possible "the goal of democracy," writes Professor R. M. MacIver, "is the remarkable differentiation and proliferation of groups—not economic alone, but religious, cultural, ethnic, and so forth, in all kinds of combination and variation—that characterize modern large-scale society." [6] This condition of freedom and democracy is resisted and condemned by the uniformitarians. "It is this condition," says MacIver, "that arouses the anachronistic fury of the totalitarians, with their instinct for primitive conformism." [7] The totalitarian strives to destroy the concept of nonlegal society in which free multi-groups exist and to force all individuals in all of their activities, particularly educational, into the law-encased and force-endowed state. Man must, under this doctrine, be totally and exclusively under the power and authority of the state; there may be no "proliferating associations that correspond to many divergent interests of modern man." [8] This is an unnatural condition for man; it is destructive of his liberty and dignity. The man who can live without society, said Aristotle, is either a beast or a god. "But the man who can live exclusively for the state," wrote MacIver, "if indeed such a being exists, is either a tyrant or a slave." [9]

Professor Alfred Whitehead, writing of freedom, maintains that "the problem of liberty has been transformed" by the development of autonomous associations. [10] He says that this method, new in the Christian era, "consists in the deliberate formation of institutions, embodying purposes of special groups, and unconcerned with the general purposes of any political state. . . ." [11] The founding of the Christian religion successfully challenged the monolithic concept of society. Within society there was to be not only the legal community (the state), but also voluntary associations enjoying autonomy.[12]

The development of self-governing institutions, declared the distinguished Cambridge professor, places the problem of liberty at a new angle. In the ancient world the political authority held exclusive power of action. In the modern world voluntary associations have "the power of action without immediate reference to the state." [13] This new autonomy of institutions is based on the claim of institutional liberty and the right to exercise control.

"This new form of liberty which is the autonomous institution limited to special purposes, was especially exemplified in the guilds of the middle ages; and that period was characterized by a remarkable growth of civilized genius," wrote Whitehead. But the "great 'liberty' which first confronted the Roman Empire," observed the English philosopher, was "the Catholic Church." "It was a standing challenge to any form of communal despotism, a universal 'liberty.' " [14]

The Christian concept of man imposes limitations on the power of government. The ideal of man's dignity and worth, of his end and purpose in life, clashes sharply with the notion of the absolute state. The Christian doctrine of man's purpose in life presupposes the right to associate himself with the autonomous Church founded by Christ. The freedom of the Church to exist as an autonomous spiritual society and the freedom of the individual person to associate himself with the Church, it should not be forgotten, were purchased with the blood of thousands of martyrs.[15] Government's recognition of the Church as an autonomous society and of the right of the individual citizen to associate himself with the Church is a recognition of the principle of limited government power. It is, in fact, a recognition of the right of the individual to give "a divided allegiance to many intersecting institutions pursuing diverse ends." [16] The development of these two basic freedoms—the freedom of the individual and the freedom of the autonomous group—is the story of freedom in Western civilization.

Within the American and English constitutional context, the individual, in the words of Professor Barker, claims "the right to think and advocate his own thoughts, to form and pursue his own tastes, and to associate himself with others for the common advocacy and the common pursuit of the thoughts and tastes which he and they share. This is a fundamental liberty; and indeed, we may find, in the issue, that it is the basis of all others." [17] Without this liberty autonomous associations established for the pursuit and communication of truth would be impossible.

This claim to liberty, maintains Barker, is based on "the assumption that in our human world, and under God, the individual personality of man alone has intrinsic and ultimate worth, and having also the capacity of development has also an intrinsic and ultimate claim to the essential development. Liberty will then be that essential condition; and the essence of liberty will be that it is a condition, or status, or quality, which individual personality must possess in order that it may translate itself from what it is to what it has the capacity of becoming." [18] In the pursuit of truth the individual person, because of his intrinsic and ultimate worth, has a right to the development of his total personality. And for this development of the total human person, including his quest of and union with Ultimate Truth, liberty is an essential condition. If the individual personality is to "translate itself from what it is to what it has the capacity of becoming," it must have the liberty to develop itself according to its essential nature. This demands an unencumbered liberty in the pursuit of truth.

This unencumbered liberty in the pursuit of truth entitles the individual to associate himself with others for the pursuit of truth and for the inquiry into the unknown. Such free association is the condition of personal development. It makes possible the free man—the man who has not been uni-formed, who has not been forced to conform to the state ideology. This is the free man. If the free man is to remain free, he must resist those who "would make the all-inclusive state the sufficient focus of our moral and spiritual being," who "would even, as totalitarians, ruthlessly co-ordinate out of existence our cultural heterogeneity." [19]

It is the individual personality that is of great importance. It is the development and growth of the individual that makes possible the development and growth of society. Society is no wiser, no more intelligent, than its constituent members. If American society is to be characterized by intellectual, cultural, moral, and religious qualities, these qualities must distinguish the individuals of our society. The community cannot rise above the merits of its constituent members. John Stuart Mill expressed this thought very cogently when he wrote that "the worth of a State, in the long run, is the worth of the individuals composing it . . . a State which dwarfs its men, in order that they may be more docile instruments in its hands even for beneficial purposes—will find that with small men no great thing can really be accomplished." [20]

The individual human person has capacities for considerable growth, if not for greatness, but this can take place only if the individual is permitted to grow as a distinctive though social personality. If the individual is submerged in the mass, "even for beneficial purposes," his individuality is destroyed and he grows not at all. He must be permitted the right to think and advocate his own thoughts. To achieve this he must be allowed to choose to associate himself with others for a number of specific purposes—educational, economic, occupational, charitable, professional, or for purely social purposes. Enforced conformity to the mass destroys individuality; the destruction of individuality achieves only the destruction of the creativeness, ingenuity, intelligence, and wisdom that must characterize any society that is not already in decay.

Enforced conformity in all aspects of life—this is the totalitarian state. It eliminates both society and the individual personality, leaving only a mass state that has engulfed and caught up every citizen into the crushing embrace of legal omnipotence. In such a state "the ultimate end of life becomes not the development of individual personality, but the exaltation of the super-personality of the State; and the cult of power is substituted for that of liberty." [21]

It cannot, therefore, be too much insisted that "the community is more than the state, that in its spontaneous life and in the rich difference it breeds there move the forces that create the future, and that for this reason the cultural values of men and groups must remain essentially free from the uniformizing activities of government." [22] If "the community is more than the state," and if "in its spontaneous life and in the rich difference it breeds there move the forces that create the future," the processes of education cannot be under the exclusive control of the state. Diversity in education is essential. When all education must conform to a state-determined philosophy, the "spontaneous life" of the community and the "rich difference it breeds" are dealt a crippling blow, and the community that is "more than the state" is deprived of its source of life, of its idealism, its individuality, and its personality. And as a consequence "the cultural values of men and groups" which "must remain essentially free from the uniformizing activities of government" are, in fact, brought under the direct uniformizing control of government through monopoly in education. State-enforced uniformity in education results in cultural uniformity. Enforced cultural uniformity means the destruction of society and of individuality. When this transpires, the individual is "created" in the image of the state rather than in the image of freedom.

The freedom enjoyed by associations is both derivative and instrumental. In the final analysis, however, "what must flow freely, and what must be free, is always man himself—the individual man—the human personality." [23] Free occupational, economic, educational, social, professional, or charitable associations are simply groups in which and by which individuals can "attain *their* freedom—the only true and ultimate freedom." [24]

It seems difficult to challenge the proposition that the freedom of associations is directly related to freedom of thought. It seems equally difficult to challenge the proposition that freedom of thought can best be assured by removing the state as far as possible from those agencies and processes which have a tremendous influence in determining what men shall think and believe.

If freedom of thought and freedom of belief are to be fully achieved, the state must not be permitted to interfere with or even, because of its dominant power, to participate in the dialogue between citizen and citizen. It was for freedom of dialogue—dialogue free of government interference—that Socrates gave his life. In this connection Whitehead writes that "Plato's own writings constituted one prolonged apology for freedom of contemplation, and for freedom for the communication of contemplative experience. In the persistent exercise of this right Socrates and Plato lived, and it was on its behalf that Socrates died." [25]

If freedom of thought is to be achieved, government must,

since freedom of thought is a guaranteed right, create those conditions that make it possible. Freedom must be capable of achievement; otherwise it cannot sustain the life-giving qualities of democracy. But if a nonconforming student's pursuit of truth is obstructed by government denial of equal educational benefits, then government is guilty of depriving him of freedom of thought. He is deprived of the right to think and investigate freely, to develop his individual personality, and to share his thoughts with his fellow citizens in the elemental process of democracy. He is deprived of what Professor Barker called "a fundamental liberty," a liberty which is "the basis of all others." This is government thought control; it circumscribes and suppresses the freedom of the individual in the pursuit of truth.

When government conditions participation in its educational benefits on the surrender of freedom of thought and freedom of belief, it is forcibly depriving citizens of these most fundamental liberties. Put in another way, when government enforces conformity to the philosophical and theological orientation of a particular school as a condition for sharing in educational benefits, it violates freedom of thought and freedom of religion.

Some very undesirable consequences result from this policy of enforced conformity. As more and more students are economically coerced to attend government schools, voluntary educational associations, which are founded on the principle of free and diversified inquiry, will become less and less important in shaping the future of America. This poses an important question in the preservation of freedom. While the vast majority of school-age Americans are economically forced to conform to the philosophical and theological orientation of state educational institutions and while, as a consequence, voluntary educational associations are exerting progressively less influence on the thought of American society, can other voluntary associations survive? Can such associations be maintained by a people that has been incubated, shaped, and formed in a system of enforced conformity? Under such circumstances, can professional, economic, occupational, charitable, cultural, and social voluntary associations—all of which are dependent for both inception and existence on free and diversified thought—continue to act autonomously and as a bulwark of freedom in America? Can voluntary associations survive once the state can, through its exclusive control of education, control what the people shall think?

It seems apparent that a state-controlled educational system cannot inspire and sustain that diversity of thought essential for a multigroup society constituted of diverse voluntary autonomous associations. In fact, John Stuart Mill warns against the negative results of state monopoly in education. He writes that "a general State education is a mere contrivance for moulding people to be exactly like one another: and . . . the mould in which it casts them is that which pleases the predominant power in the government . . . ; in proportion as it is efficient and successful, it establishes a despotism over the mind, leading by natural tendency to one over the body." [26]

Even if we discount Mill's convictions regarding the purpose and results of state monopoly in education, there can be little doubt that such a system of education will not inspire that diversity of thought necessary for a free society and, more particularly, for a system of competitive business and free enterprise. The diversity of education required by the American system of free enterprise quite obviously has no place in the USSR where the production and distribution of goods, like the schools, are government monopolies. On the contrary, diversity in education is required by the many and varied facets of American society.

Diversity in education is a necessary prerequisite for freedom of thought and freedom of inquiry; it makes possible the active exercise of those freedoms and those responsibilities that characterize a free society. It enables the student to undertake the pursuit of truth open-mindedly and to draw his conclusions on the basis of evidence; he is not forced to conform to an educational philosophy that arbitrarily censors vast areas of knowledge. Diversity in education, moreover, enables the student to make free choices in the pursuit of truth. To make choices is man's highest perfection. When the state denies this right, it maims and stunts his personality; it violates the most fundamental of his freedoms. Compulsory conformity to a state-charted course in pursuit of truth is not only inconsistent with the freedom of the human mind, but it is also inconsistent with the principles and needs of a multigroup society.

If the modern problem of liberty is, as Professor Whitehead so eloquently maintains, inextricably related to the development and preservation of voluntary associations, then our most important task is to find ways and means of preserving our multigroup society from strangulation by state power. If the state, by direct or indirect action, eliminates all voluntary associations, we shall have an absolute state. And all our institutional activities shall orbit like satellites around the all-inclusive state.

The autonomy of voluntary associations can, in the long view, best be secured, inasmuch as this is possible, by assuring to every child (through his parents) and to every student freedom of thought in education. And freedom of thought in education can, in turn, best be achieved by freedom of choice in schooling. In the American context this requires a diversity of schools. And this diversity of educational opportunities must be available to our children and their parents on the basis of a "free choice." That is, the exercise of choice in education may not be penalized by a denial of educational benefits. When the granting of educational benefits is conditioned on the choice of a particular kind of education, the state is coercing conformity to this particular orientation of truth. This is a violation of freedom of thought and destructive of diversity in education.[27]

Such compulsory state action will inevitably lead, because of the mounting cost of schooling, to virtual state monopoly in education. Against this our society must gird itself for the sake of liberty. "Educational associations," writes Professor Barker, "may contribute greatly to the solution of the ancient problem of liberty." Voluntary societies which engage in the education of the young are necessary, he argues, since the field of education "is not, and never can be, a monopoly of the State. Educational associations—of parents, of teachers, of workers, and of members of religious confessions—are all concerned in the development of educational experiments, and in offering that liberty of choice among types of school and forms of instruction which is essential to the growth of personal and individual capacity." [28]

There is general agreement, it is hoped, with the proposition adopted by the Commission on Financing Higher Education, that a diversity of educational institutions is necessary for the preservation of liberty. "What most protects freedom of choice in America is the great diversity of its institutions, none of which possesses overriding power. . . . Human beings and their institutions being what they are, total power is not safe in the hand of any single group no matter how well intentioned," declared the Commission.[29]

The problem of maintaining a diversity of education in America is a serious one. It is a problem that cannot be solved by independent educational institutions alone. It is not, in fact, their problem at all. The problem belongs to American society. And it is a problem that our society will have to solve if we are to secure the freedom of thought essential to democracy.

Education from the elementary grades through the graduate school is a costly item. It is one for which only a small percentage of our parents can afford to pay. Yet because of our democratic ideals, we insist that every child is entitled to all the education of which he is capable. Who shall pay for it? Since society is the secondary beneficiary of the education of the young, the state has, in every nation, undertaken to subsidize the education of its children.

In subsidizing the education of their children, nations have adopted one of three broad policies. First, they have adopted a policy of freedom of thought and freedom of belief. They subsidize the education of all children in the schools of their choice. Second, they have adopted a policy of coercive conformity to the philosophical and theological orientation of state educational institutions. They subsidize the education of only those children who conform by attending government schools. Nonconforming students are denied all educational subsidies. Third, they have adopted a policy of compulsory conformity to state educational doctrines through *compulsory* attendance at government schools. They also subsidize the education of all children.

Compulsory conformity to state educational doctrines is the policy adopted by every totalitarian state. The state that sets out to control every aspect of the lives of its people takes a giant step, and an essential step, in this direction by thought control through its educational system.

Nearly every democracy in the West has adopted a policy of freedom of thought and freedom of belief in education. Our nation stands virtually alone among democracies in adopting a general policy of coercive conformity to the philosophical and theological orientation of government education as a condition for sharing in state educational benefits.

This constitutes one of our major educational problems in America. While the several states yearly spend more than $300 for the education of each child and more than $1,000 for the education of each college student who conforms to government educational policy, they deprive all nonconformist students of all educational subsidies.

When these students, deprived of state educational benefits and, for the most part, unable to pay the actual cost of education, seek admission to independent schools, these schools have two alternatives. First, they can require that the student pay the full cost of education. This would be equivalent to barring the doors of independent education to the vast majority of students who seek admission. Such students, with the exception of scholarship winners, would, consequently, be forced to conform to state educational policy as the only alternative to no education. This alternative would, in effect, make of our independent educational institutions empty castles of learning inhabited only by the ghosts of academic freedom. There is no future for independent education in pricing itself out of business.

The second alternative for independent schools is to fix tuition at a level within the reach of a sufficient number of students, or their parents, to enable the institutions to continue the work of education. In practice this means charging tuition that amounts to half or less than half the actual cost of education. This policy results in operational deficits which, on the college level, frequently run into many hundreds of thousands of dollars. It results, moreover, in low faculty salaries, in inadequate facilities, in lack of research opportunities, and in a score of other economy limitations that impede the process of education.

The financial problems that threaten the survival, or at least encumber the educational activities, of a large majority of America's independent schools are directly consequent upon state educational policy which subsidizes the student's education in public institutions but not in independent institutions. In the educational market place, this puts the independent schools in the difficult competitive position of having to compete with highly subsidized government schools. The competitive position of independent schools is analogous to that of the corner grocery store which tries to compete with well-supplied government owned and operated supermarkets that sell their merchandise at an 80 or 90 per cent discount. No businessman, no matter what the quality of his goods and the excellence of his services, could long survive such a disadvantageous competitive situation. Yet this is precisely the situation that confronts independent educational institutions.

In economic terms what is happening is quite simple. In the educational market place there are two types of institutions. They are government or independent, depending on whether they are controlled by government or by voluntary associations. In this market place government has undertaken to subsidize the *supply* of education—but only the state supply. Government subsidizes only state educational institutions. The independent supply of education is not subsidized.

The policy of subsidizing only the government supply of education places the state in the position of exercising thought control. Freedom of thought would seem to demand that government subsidize also the independent supply of education, thus giving students freedom of choice in schooling.

Competent scholars have advanced the proposition that government should limit its role in education exclusively to subsidizing the *demand*, that is, the student. This plan proposes that government should subsidize the individual student with a certificate of money value and give him complete freedom of choice in purchasing his schooling in the market place of education.[30] Under this proposal there would be no government-controlled educational institutions.

On the other hand, there seems to be no good reason why government should not, in fulfilling its educational obligations under state and Federal constitutions, subsidize both the supply and the demand. In subsidizing government educational institutions, it is subsidizing the supply, and in subsidizing the individual independent school student it would subsidize the demand. Such a policy would not only eliminate the dire prospect of complete state monopoly in education, but would also assure a considerable measure of freedom of thought consequent upon freedom of choice. It is the writer's purpose to advance reasons in favor of the adoption of such an educational policy by the several states and, to the extent that the Federal Government enters the field of education, by the Federal Government. This policy could be implemented either by a tax credit, or by the granting of a certificate of money value, to the parents of students who attend independent or out-state government schools. The reasons advanced in support of freedom of choice in education are equally valid for the tax credit plan and for the certificate plan.

The certificate plan received a new impetus several years ago when two University of Chicago professors, in separate articles, proposed the plan.[31] Professor Milton Friedman wrote: "Governments . . . could finance [education] by giving parents vouchers redeemable for a specified maximum sum per child per year if spent on 'approved' educational services. Parents would then be free to spend this sum and any additional sum on purchasing educational services from an 'approved' institution of their own choice. The educational services could be rendered by private enterprises operated for profit, or by non-profit institutions of various kinds." [32]

Professor Friedman declared that the proposed voucher or

certificate plan has good precedent not only in the United States but also in Great Britain and France. He pointed out that "an excellent example of a program of this sort is the United States educational program for veterans after World War II. Each veteran who qualified was given a maximum sum per year that could be spent at any institution of his choice, provided it met certain standards. A more limited example is the provision in Britain whereby local authorities pay the fees of some students attending non-state schools (the so-called 'public schools'). Another is the arrangement in France whereby the state pays part of the costs for students attending non-state schools." [33]

Professor Procter Thomson, writing in *The School Review*, raises a question that is elemental in a democracy, and he gives the answer that the freedom of a democratic society demands. He wrote: "Must schools be publicly administered? It is obvious that free schools and public administration can easily be separated by two devices, one of which would subsidize the supply of education, the other of which would subsidize the demand. A public grant could be given to privately operated schools as such, or a certificate could be issued to the individual family which it would be free to spend at a school of its own choosing. The school would then exchange the certificate for an equivalent sum of money." [34]

Freedom of choice in education is made possible by government grants to independent schools or by grants to individual students which may take the form of certificates. "The second alternative," points out Professor Thomson, "has the merit of allowing the direct exercise of individual preferences to determine what types of schools would best service their interests." [35]

This plan recently received the approval of the American Association of Land-Grant Colleges and State Universities. At its 1956 annual meeting, the Association went on record as favoring in principle Federal grants to individual students on the undergraduate and graduate levels. The resolution adopted by the Association incorporated the principle of freedom of choice in education. Among other things, the resolution proposed that (1) payments be made to individuals, (2) that no restrictions be made as to accredited institution attended, and (3) that the student be free to choose any areas of subject matter desired.[36]

There is a rapidly growing interest in the tax credit plan. Committees, educational groups, and Congressmen have recommended this plan in recent months. The President's Committee on Education Beyond the High School recommended in its Second Report that "the Federal revenue laws be revised . . . in ways which will permit deductions or credits on income tax returns by students, their parents or others who contribute to meeting the expenditures necessarily incurred in obtaining formal education beyond high school. . . ."[37]

The Association of American Colleges in its January, 1958, meeting adopted a resolution calling upon Congress to enact legislation providing a "tax credit on individual incomes for tuition fee payments."[38] The American Council on Education has proposed a tax credit plan to give a "tax relief" for "student tuition and fees paid to tax-exempt public and private educational institutions."[39]

More than a score of bills have been introduced in Congress providing for a tax credit for tuition and fees paid to public or private institutions of higher education. Typical of such bills are those introduced in the 85th Congress by Congressman Eugene J. McCarthy of Minnesota (H.R. 765) and Congressman Hale Boggs of Louisiana (H.R. 1064) which provide for a 30 per cent credit against the individual income tax for amounts paid as tuition and fees to public and private institutions of higher education, or at a level above the twelfth grade. Congressman Melvin R. Laird of Wisconsin, however, introduced a bill providing for a tax credit for the tuition and fees paid to both colleges and high schools. The Laird bill, like the others, does not provide a credit for the full amount of the tuition and fees. It also calls for a 30 per cent credit.

Since the certificate or tax credit plan would enable parents and students to pay tuition approximating the cost of education at the school of their choice, it would make possible the development of strong and healthy voluntary educational associations—thus establishing a bulwark of freedom against the powers of government. Professor Thomson observes that "on general grounds and with other things the same, it is evident that publicly financed, privately operated free education, with individual choice as to type of school attended, would be a highly desirable arrangement within the liberal-democratic frame of reference. It would reduce the power of government, an agency of social choice in indirect or delegated form, and increase the range of direct individual choice. . . . This proposal is not without justification on grounds of social policy and economic efficiency." [40]

American society demands diversity in education. "The hallmark of freedom," observed Dr. A. Whitney Griswold, president of Yale University, in a baccalaureate address, "is diversity." [41] The multigroup structure of our society is based on freedom of thought and freedom of belief. The tax credit or certificate plan, making possible freedom of choice in education, would guarantee that freedom of inquiry and freedom of investigation which are essential for a society of voluntary associations striving to achieve their particular goals and to maintain their independence from government control.

The tax credit or certificate plan, moreover, would secure the right of the individual to share equally in government educational benefits regardless of thought or belief. And it would accomplish this worthy objective, as we shall see, consistent with the principles of both state and Federal constitutions.

# 2

# Constitutionality of Direct
# Educational Subsidies
# to Students

*The certificate or tax credit plan of direct government educational subsidies to the individual child or student does not raise constitutional questions.*

The problem confronting most of the states that might wish to support religious schools is lodged in their constitutions and in judicial decisions. The constitutions of a considerable majority of the states contain prohibitions against the use of public money in support of denominational schools.[1] The "no establishment" clause of the First Amendment to the Federal Constitution, as recently reinterpreted by the Supreme Court of the United States in the *Everson* and *McCollum* cases, moreover, prohibits all government aid to religion or religious institutions.[2]

Mid-twentieth century Americans like to believe that they have outgrown the religious animosities and prejudices that, more than a century ago, poisoned the political seedbed from which sprang the constitutional amendments prohibiting the use of public funds in support of religious schools. With few exceptions, these amendments were adopted by the then existing states during periods of intense anti-Catholic agitation and periods that witnessed the bloody and destructive religious riots against the Catholic minority. These riots were the direct result of the "school controversy" which arose out of the enforced study of the Protestant religion by Catholic children in public schools that were in fact in every sense Protestant schools.[3] This practice gave rise to Catholic demands for public support of independent schools and/or permission allowing Catholic children to absent themselves from Protestant religious instructions. These demands, consistent with both justice and liberty, were enough, in a sociological context in which the publication of anti-Catholic literature was big business and the topic of almost every Sunday sermon was Popery, to ignite the smoldering hostility against Catholics which resulted in scores of citizens killed, dozens of churches burned, and more than a hundred homes destroyed.[4]

This was the seedbed from which sprang the constitutional amendments which, even in the more tolerant atmosphere of the mid-twentieth century, prohibit the support of religious schools. "The drive to prevent assistance by the state to Catholic parochial schools, stimulated by periodic anti-Catholic movements," writes Professor Robert Cushman, "led to the adoption of [prohibitory] provisions in nearly every state."[5]

Dr. Bernard Iddings Bell, Episcopalian clergyman and scholar, referring to this period of American history, writes that "Catholics demanded that the [state] schools should teach to Catholic children religion as Catholics understand it. If this could not be done, they demanded a share of school tax money wherewith to run their own schools. Why, they asked, should all the cash go to schools that taught Protestantism of one sort or another? Both these demands were denied."[6]

Describing this situation a Protestant writer says that "when the Roman Catholics appeared in numbers sufficient to demand, with some possibility of success, that they be not subjected to what they considered a sectarian Protestant religious education, and that in lieu of that they be given money for parochial schools for the teaching of Catholic doctrines, a rising tide of Nationalism united the Protestant sects to provide in the fundamental law against a possible use of state money intended for common schools, in sectarian schools which were not in the regularly administered system of common schools. But it was more a matter of expediency than principle, *for care was taken to exclude colleges from the prohibition.*" [7]

Although the vast majority of Americans, truly dedicated to the principles of the Bill of Rights, may desire, like the citizens of virtually all other Western democracies, to support religious schools, these constitutional provisions and the Supreme Court's *Everson* doctrine of *absolute* separation of church and state apparently make this unfeasible at the present time.

It should be pointed out, however, that although the prejudices of a period of history have fixed the words of the several state constitutions and the "prepossessions" of the Supreme Court, as Justice Jackson candidly admitted, have fixed the meaning of the "no establishment" clause of the First Amendment, they cannot set limits to a growing spirit of tolerance and to a new recognition of the equal rights of the individual regardless of race, color, or religious belief.

Ignoring the prejudices that permeated the nineteenth century, state courts now generally hold that there is no constitutional prohibition against payments, on a contract basis, to educational institutions under denominational control for services rendered in the education of youth, particularly when such payments are less than the cost of education. This principle was enunciated, for example, in the *Chicago Industrial School* case in which the Supreme Court of Illinois declared that "it is contrary to fact and reason to say that paying less than the actual cost of clothing, medical care and attention, education and training in useful arts and domestic science, is aiding the institution where such things are furnished." [8] This is the payment-for-value-received principle. The court went on to make the not too profound observation that "it is the State, and not the industrial school, that is benefited by the payment of less than the cost of food, clothing, medical care and attention and education and training in the useful arts and domestic science." On the basis of this reasoning, the court held that "upon the plainest grounds no aid is given to an industrial school where the payment is less than the actual cost, aside from and regardless of any religious instruction or religious exercise." [9]

State governments are today subsidizing the education of only those children and students who attend state educational institutions, except for several states which give freedom of choice to scholarship winners. The education of each child in the public schools is subsidized, on the average, to the extent of about $310 a year. The education of each state university student is subsidized to the extent of roughly $900 to $1,100 a year, or more. But, on the other hand, children and young men and women who attend independent educational institutions receive no educational subsidy whatsoever. The certificate and tax credit plans are methods by which government can subsidize their education, at least in part.

These plans raise no constitutional questions. The certificate plan provides that government make direct money grants in the form of vouchers or certificates to parents or guardians of all children attending approved independent schools. A voucher or certificate of $150, for example, would be valid when used in partial payment of tuition and signed by a parent or guardian and school principal. Under this plan government could also give vouchers or certificates of $500, for example, to college students to enable them to pay in part tuition and fees at independent institutions, or at government institutions in other than the student's state of residence. The plan is identical in principle with Federal money grants to veterans for the payment of tuition and fees in the schools of their choice.

The tax credit plan, on the other hand, provides that government give a tax offset to parents of all children attending approved independent tuition-charging schools. A tax credit or offset of $150, for example, could be given to parents and guardians for each child attending an independent school for whom they pay tuition in excess of $150. Under this plan government could also give a tax credit of $500, for example, to parents or guardians, or to students themselves, to enable them to pay in part tuition and fees at independent institutions, or at government institutions in other than the student's state of residence.

Recent proposals for a tax credit for parents to enable them to send their children to the school of their choice do not provide for a lump-sum credit but rather a credit covering a certain per cent of the tuition and fees. The formula suggested by the Resolutions Committee of the Taxation Section of the American Bar Association at its 1954 convention, for example, "provides that 30 per cent of student tuition and fees actually paid by the taxpayer to the institution be applied as a tax credit on the amount of income tax otherwise payable." [10] All tuition-paying taxpayers would receive the same tax benefits in dollars, regardless of whether they are in the 20 per cent, 50 per cent, or 91 per cent income tax bracket.

The tax credit plan should be clearly distinguished from the tax deduction plan. If the tuition is $800, for example, what tax benefits would the two plans give to parents who pay the tuition of their children? If the parent is in the 20 per cent bracket, he would, under the tax deduction plan, save $160 of taxes; if he is in the 50 per cent bracket he would save $400 of taxes. Under a tax credit plan providing for a 30 per

cent credit of tuition and fees, on the other hand, the parent
in the 20 per cent bracket and the parent in the 50 per cent
bracket would be given equal tax relief. They would both be
given a tax offset of $240 (30 per cent of $800). This amount
would be subtracted from their personal tax bills.

Since the Federal Government does not operate a Federal
"free" school system through which it subsidizes the education of attending students, any Federal tax credit program to
aid college-level students might well extend the credit to all
students regardless of school attended, government or independent.

From this analysis, it is clear that the certificate or tax credit
plan involves no government aid or support of church-related
schools. The government subsidy is given directly to parents
to enable them to pay in part their children's tuition at the
school of their choice. Parents and their children alone are
the beneficiaries of the subsidy.

The certificate or tax credit plan is designed to enable parents or students to pay a greater percentage of the cost of education. It does not propose to aid the school of the parent's or
student's choice. The President's Committee on Education
Beyond the High School observed, in discussing the G.I. bill,
that it "does not believe that this assistance to veterans was
designed to help, even *indirectly*, the institutions. Actually it
imposed an enormous burden on them, a burden they accepted as a part of their mission in our society, but a heavy
financial and administrative burden nonetheless." [11] When
government helps parents and students pay *part* of a tuition
which is itself considerably less than the cost of education at
the school attended, no reasonable person would contend that
government is subsidizing the school. The school, as the President's Committee pointed out, actually assumes an "enormous burden" in its efforts to promote the welfare of society.
The school is not only not subsidized, but the school itself

subsidizes the education of government subsidized students.

It is fundamental that the state's educational obligations are not to *institutions* and *systems*; its obligations are to *children*—the individual children of the state. Educational institutions and systems are but *means* to help the state carry out its educational obligations. This means (the institutions) is not, however, coextensive with the state's obligations.

The state's obligations in the matter of education extend to each individual child and student. And these obligations must be fulfilled consistent with the guarantees of positive personal rights and within the limits of restrictions imposed by the Federal Constitutions. In a totalitarian state, the government can force all children to attend public educational institutions. In a democracy, on the other hand, in which freedom of mind and religion are protected by the Constitution, the government may not force children to attend state schools.

A government may, indeed, establish a state school system. But since it cannot coerce attendance, constitutional guarantees demand that it seek other means to fulfill its educational obligations to children and students who, for philosophical or theological reasons, cannot conform to the established philosophical and theological orientation of state schools. This duty is incumbent on the state since it cannot demand the surrender of the constitutional right to attend an independent school or college as a condition for sharing in welfare benefits. The constitution compels the state to employ such means to secure a child's or student's education as are not incompatible with his rights under the Constitution.

The certificate or tax credit plan enables the several states to fulfill their obligations to children and students in independent schools and colleges within the limits of existing constitutional provisions. The subsidy is given directly to parents. And parents, exercising freedom of choice, select the kind of education they want for their children in the open market of education. In this plan parents of children and students attending independent schools and colleges would pay tuition charges in part with government issued certificates or tax credits. Thus the schools would in no way be subsidized with public funds; only parents and their children would be subsidized.

The certificate or tax credit plan is in principle the same as the plans the Federal Government adopted to enable veterans, war orphans, and the pages of Congress to get an education at the school of their choice. The direct subsidy principle, incorporating the principle of freedom of choice, was adopted, in one form or another, in the Servicemen's Readjustment Act of 1944, the Veterans' Readjustment Act of 1952, the War Orphans' Educational Assistance Act of 1956, and in the educational provisions of the Legislative Reorganization Act of 1946 for the education of the pages of Congress.

The Federal Government subsidized the education of World War II veterans by directly paying tuition and fees of the individual veteran at the school of his choice. The government subsidized the education of Korean veterans by directly subsidizing the individual veteran to enable him to pay tuition and fees at the school of his choice. And, finally, the government is subsidizing the education of war orphans by directly subsidizing the individual student to enable him to pay tuition and fees at the school of his choice.

Individual veterans, with government subsidy in hand, paid tuition, fees, and incidental charges at one or other of our 481 nonsectarian, 474 Protestant, 265 Catholic, and 5 Jewish institutions of higher learning, or at one of our state colleges or universities. The college the veteran elected to attend not only received no government subsidy, but the college itself, since tuition does not pay for the educational costs, subsidized the veteran's education.

In this way the Federal Government has paid out many

millions of dollars for the education of veterans in non-sectarian colleges and universities and in the colleges and universities of the several religious denominations. As a matter of fact, the government has spent millions of dollars for the education of no fewer than 36,000 veterans studying to become ministers of religion, most of them Protestants.

The beneficiaries of these expenditures, as we have seen, are the individual students; consequently, the constitutional question of separation of church and state cannot properly be raised. The principle that the state can subsidize the individual citizen without subsidizing the religion to which he adheres or the religious organizations to which he belongs has been repeatedly enunciated by the Supreme Court of the United States. A state may, for example, give textbooks to children attending church-related schools. "The schools," said the Court, "are not the beneficiaries of these appropriations. They obtain nothing from them, nor are they relieved of a single obligation, because of them. The school children and the state alone are the beneficiaries." [12] A state may also subsidize parents to help them transport their children to the school of their choice, even though the school be church-related. When such grants are made to parents, declared the Court, "the State contributes no money to the schools. It does not support them. Its legislation, as applied, does no more than provide a general program to help parents get their children, regardless of their religion, safely and expeditiously to and from accredited schools." [13]

This principle of equality of treatment for believers flows of necessity from the constitutional guarantee of religious liberty. If it were otherwise, a citizen would become, by reason of his religious belief, a second-class citizen. The First Amendment guarantees that religious belief shall not be cause for civil disabilities and for degradation to the level of second-class citizenship. Thomas Jefferson, the great exponent of civil liberties, emphasized this principle when he declared that "our civil rights have no dependence on our religious opinions." [14]

The two principles incorporated in the certificate plan are identical with those incorporated in the old-age assistance program. First, in both the certificate plan and the old-age assistance program, government subsidizes the demand; it does not subsidize the supply. Second, in both, the individual who is subsidized is given complete freedom of choice to purchase particular needs in the open market place.

Government subsidizes the *demand* when it gives to individual citizens a money subsidy to purchase the commodity or commodities which the government, through its taxing power, is making available to a class of citizens. The subsidized individual citizen is given complete freedom of choice in purchasing the particular commodity or commodities in the open market.

Government subsidizes the *supply* when it subsidizes particular stores, or itself operates government stores, to supply a particular commodity or commodities to a particular class of individuals. The individuals for whom these benefits are intended have no freedom of choice. They have no alternative; they must accept the commodities provided by the government or they go without.

Not so many years ago the aged in need of government assistance were forced to go to state institutions for the needs of life. There they were compelled to accept the kind of meals, the kind of service, the kind of clothing the institutions provided. Freedom of choice in these matters was, for all practical purposes, non-existent.

Today, however, in keeping with our respect for the dignity of the individual person, we have emancipated the needy aged from such government control over their physical needs. We have not done this by setting up government stores to distribute to the needy aged certain government selected brands of food and certain government selected fashions of clothing. This method, though it would relieve the aged of institutionalized living, would, nevertheless, still maintain complete government control over what the aged shall eat and what they shall wear. They would have no freedom of choice; their diet and apparel would be determined by government officials. There is unquestionably a servitude involved in the acceptance of such services and goods from the hands of government. It is incompatible with the dignity of the human person.

We have accomplished the emancipation of the needy aged by directly subsidizing the individual person. We subsidize the demand. And the subsidized citizen is free to exercise his prerogative of choice in the purchase of his needs in the open market place.

The subsidized aged person may choose to purchase personally all of his needs and to live alone or with his family. Or he may choose to spend his subsidy to pay for subsistence with relatives or friends. Or, again, he may choose to spend the subsidy to pay for subsistence at some home for the aged operated by a particular religious group.

Under the old-age assistance program, thousands of our needy aged men and women have chosen to purchase their subsistent needs at denominational institutions. This purchase is made with money supplied by the Federal and state governments. In making this purchase in such institutions, they are exercising the freedom of choice guaranteed by the Social Security Act.

It is sometimes objected that the certificate method of subsidizing the education of children would involve government control of the schools the children choose to attend. This objection is based on the supposition that government control invariably follows the government dollar.

The objection can probably be best answered by an analysis of government activities in other programs in which it subsidizes the individual citizen.

When individual needy aged men and women purchase their needs at denominational institutions, does the government subsidize such institutions? If so, are the institutions subject to government control? These questions can, perhaps, most readily be answered by posing another question. When millions of individual needy aged men and women, using government subsidies, buy the needs of life at thousands of different private stores and shops throughout the nation, does the government subsidize these business enterprises? If so, are Macy's, Gimbels, Borden, the A&P, and Swift subject to government control?

The individual needy aged may take his government subsidy and shop with complete freedom. The subsidy is not conditioned on the surrender of the freedom to purchase the physical needs of life wherever he prefers. Furthermore, the aged person may purchase whatever he desires. If for reasons of religious belief he does not wish to eat pork, it is not forced upon him by an intolerant government operating a government meat shop. The individual may purchase kosher meat, or he may purchase fish, or he may choose to dine exclusively on a vegetable diet; this is a personal matter and the government will not attempt to control his diet.

In 1955 the Federal Government and the several states subsidized the needy aged to the extent of $1,589,802,000. In that year 2,548,593 men and women received an average of $52.30 a month under the old-age program.[15] This monthly subsidy is given to the individual person; it is not given to the store or market or denominational institution at which the individual needy aged purchases the commodities necessary for life.

The method adopted for providing for the needs of the aged

men and women of our nation has a care for the dignity of
their person and the independence of their individuality. They
are not forcibly coerced to eat from a government table as
a condition for sharing in government benefits.

The Federal Government subsidized the demand in another
program adopted during the depression years of the 1930's.
The government undertook to subsidize persons on relief to
enable them to buy surplus foods. Relief clients could buy
orange-colored stamps that could be used at a grocery store
for the purchase of any kind of food. When he made the
purchase of orange-colored stamps, he was *given* half as many
blue-colored stamps which could be used for the purchase of
goods in surplus. For every dollar that the citizen spent on
food, the government gave him a half-dollar for the purchase
of surplus food at the grocery of his choice.

When the government paid the grocer cash for both the
orange and blue stamps that he had collected, did it subsidize
the store? Here as in other welfare legislation the subsidy was
made directly to the individual citizen. The government did
not subsidize the hundreds of thousands of private grocery
stores across the nation. It subsidized the demand; it did not
subsidize the supply.

If it should ever be established in law that in public welfare
legislation government control follows the public dollar, then
we shall have gone a long way in setting up a totalitarian
government. The government would then exercise control over
a large portion of our private and corporate retail businesses.
The Federal and state governments would not only exercise
control over all the stores and shops at which approximately
2,600,000 needy aged spend the Federal-state dollar. But,
using 1955 data, they would also control all the stores and
shops at which the families or guardians of 2,239,430 dependent children spend a total of $620,545,000, at which
103,906 needy blind persons spend $69,253,000, and at which

236,840 permanently and totally disabled persons spend $147,093,000 Federal-state dollars.[16]

Does government have the right to control the private stores and shops at which the needy aged, the parents or guardians of dependent children, and the needy blind purchase with government subsidies, food, clothing, shelter, and other essential needs of life? True, the question sounds fantastic. Yet this is the logic of those who object to the certificate or tax credit plan on the grounds that a government subsidy for the individual child or student is a subsidy of the school attended and that such a subsidy would involve government control of independent schools.

Government control over the processes of education is infinitely more objectionable than government control of businesses which supply the physical needs of life. If forced to choose between two so great evils as government control, on the one hand, of the kind and quality of food one must eat, and, on the other hand, of the kind and quality of thoughts one must think, surely no American with a sense of the importance of freedom of thought would hesitate in making his choice. Freedom can survive, to a considerable degree, even if government tells the citizen what brand of food he must eat and what fashion of clothes he must wear. But freedom cannot long survive when government tells him what thoughts he must think.

The philosophy that government control invariably follows the public dollar would destroy academic freedom. All universities receiving government grants for scientific and medical research would, a fortiori, fall under government control. All colleges and universities admitting veterans and war orphans would likewise fall under government control. And all colleges and universities admitting Federal fellowship and scholarship winners, if there are to be such, would also fall under government control.

The American people rejected this statist philosophy when they adopted legislation establishing both our social security programs and our educational and research programs.

The doctrine that government control invariably follows the public dollar is not a valid objection to the certificate plan. This doctrine has been rejected in all our social security programs, in all our educational programs for veterans, and, recently, in our educational program for war orphans. And since freedom of the mind must be preserved, it must be rejected in future legislation in the field of education.

The reason for the rejection of this doctrine is apparent. These programs do not subsidize private business, they do not subsidize independent educational institutions; they subsidize the individual needy aged, the individual veteran, the individual war orphan. In a word, they do not subsidize the supply; they subsidize the demand. For this reason, also, as the President's Committee on Education Beyond the High School pointed out, the tax credit plan (and the same holds for the certificate plan) could be adopted "without raising the legal issue of 'church-state' relations." [17]

Consequently, the certificate and tax credit plans, like these programs, do not raise constitutional questions. Any contention to the contrary is inconsistent with both law and practice.

# 3

# The Significance of
# Freedom of Choice
# in Education

*The certificate or tax credit plan ensures freedom of choice in education.*

Freedom of choice in education is the exercise of freedom of mind and freedom of religion. Under the personal subsidy plan, parents and college students are free to choose a school on the basis of their philosophical and theological convictions. Thus children and students would not be forced to conform to the philosophical and theological orientation of state schools as a condition for sharing in public educational benefits.

Enforced conformity to state educational philosophy as a condition for sharing in educational benefits is in conflict with our two most fundamental constitutional liberties—freedom of mind and freedom of religion. The child or student is forced to surrender his freedom of thought and his freedom of belief in the choice of school; he is compelled to conform to the philosophical and theological orientation of the state's schools.

Every educational institution is philosophically and theologically oriented. There is no such thing as philosophical and theological neutrality. Since the purpose of education is to educate the human person, education cannot be neutral about the nature of the person being educated and the purpose of the person's existence. In the process of education the questions "What is man?" "Where does he come from?" "What is his purpose?" cannot be avoided. It is impossible even to attempt to answer these questions without raising the question of whether there is a God and, if so, what is man's relation to Him? Mere silence on these important questions is not neutrality.

Neutrality regarding these fundamental issues is impossible. This point is cogently made by Henry P. Van Dusen, president of Union Theological Seminary, in his *God in Education* when he says that "the gravest secularization of American education has not been in the gradual elimination of religious instruction or required chapel, or even in the irreligious outlook of faculties. It has been the secularization of educational theory and structure. Their covert assumptions concerning the two basic factors with which they have to deal—truth and man—have been non-religious. And they have been false." [1] When educators attempt to discuss "truth and man" without reference to God, this is the "non-religious" approach to the two most basic factors in education. This approach constitutes a philosophical and theological orientation vis-à-vis God and man. It is positivistic and secularistic.

Sir Walter Moberly, formerly chairman of the University Grants Committee of England, is in complete agreement with this analysis of modern education. In his book *The Crisis in the University*, Sir Walter analyzes the approach of the modern university to the question of God and concludes not only that the university is in a sense "atheistic" but that it teaches the relative unimportance of religion. He writes:

On the fundamental religious issue, the modern university intends to be, and supposes it is, neutral, but it is not. Certainly it neither inculcates nor expressly repudiates belief in God. But it does what is far more deadly than open rejection; it ignores Him. . . . It is in this sense that the university today is atheistic. . . . It is a fallacy to suppose that by omitting a subject you teach nothing about it. On the contrary you teach that it is to be omitted, and that it is therefore a matter of secondary importance. And you teach this not openly and explicitly, which would invite criticism; you simply take it for granted and thereby insinuate it silently, insidiously, and all but irresistibly. . . .[2]

If our American universities and schools ignore God and if by so doing they "insinuate . . . silently, insidiously, and all but irresistibly" that He is to be omitted, they are philosophically and theologically oriented. If, on the other hand, our public universities and schools admit a God and if they emphasize the transcendent importance of a knowledge of God and man's relations to God, they are philosophically and theologically oriented. *Whatever the philosophical and theological orientation of our state-controlled educational institutions, the child and student cannot be forced to conform to it.* This is fundamental to freedom of the mind and freedom of religion.

This elemental but basic principle of freedom was unanimously upheld by the United States Supreme Court in the well-known Oregon school case.[3] To deny this principle is to espouse the doctrine of the totalitarian state; the doctrine of compulsory conformity to the will of the state in every aspect of our lives. It is to make the child, in the words of the Supreme Court, "the mere creature of the state,"[4] to be nurtured, and fed, and trained, and taught exclusively by the all-powerful, the all-competent, the absolute state.

Democracy supposes a free people—a people who can think, and speak, and believe, and write, and assemble without government interference. And freedom means the right to be different; the right of nonconformity. It means that government may not force its citizens to conform, whether it be in speech, in belief, or in thought. It means that government may use neither direct nor indirect means to force children and students to conform to the ideological orientation of state educational institutions.

That government may not condition participation in its benefits and privileges on the surrender of constitutional rights —this is a most fundamental principle of constitutional liberty. For "if the state may compel the surrender of one constitutional right as a condition of its favor," declared the Supreme Court of the United States, "it may, in like manner, compel a surrender of all." [5] This would enable every state in the nation, as well as the Federal Government, to force citizens to surrender rights and liberties guaranteed in the Bill of Rights as a condition for sharing in the privileges and benefits provided by government to a class to which they belong. This would enable governments to do by indirection what they can not do by direct action. That is, they could in this manner arbitrarily deprive citizens of their constitutional rights. Legally, this may not be done. "It is inconceivable," said the Court, "that guaranties embedded in the Constitution of the United States may thus be manipulated out of existence." [6]

The Supreme Court of the United States, adhering to the fundamental principle that governments may not force citizens by indirection to surrender their constitutional rights, declared that a state "may not impose conditions [for sharing in benefits] which require the relinquishment of constitutional rights." [7] Mr. Justice Frankfurter reaffirmed this constitutional principle a quarter of a century later when, concurring in the *Douds* case, he declared: "Congress may withhold all sorts of facilities for a better life, but if it affords them it cannot make them available in an obviously arbitrary way or exact surrender of freedoms unrelated to the purpose of the facilities." [8]

In this day of increasing public welfare benefits, it is important that governments not be permitted to enforce conformity to a prevailing ideology as a condition for sharing in such benefits. Enforced conformity, whether achieved by direct action or by indirection, is incompatible with constitutional guarantees and with the principles of democracy. Mr. Alanson Willcox, formerly General Counsel of the Federal Security Agency, in his article on the "Invasions of the First Amendment Through Conditioned Public Spending" writes: "Whenever a state imposes a choice between . . . receiving a public benefit, on the one hand, and exercising one's constitutional freedoms, on the other, the state burdens each course to the extent that abandonment of the other is unpalatable. The deterrent to exercise of first amendment freedoms when [public benefits are] at stake is a real one. . . . Infringement of constitutional rights is nonetheless infringement because accomplished through a conditioning of a privilege." [9]

Now, it is my contention that, in the distribution of educational benefits, the several states violate this fundamental constitutional principle. In their educational policy the states demand, as a condition for sharing in educational benefits, the surrender of a constitutional right. Specifically, the states demand the surrender of freedom of mind and freedom of religion. This is to say, the states demand the surrender of freedom of choice in education. They demand that a child or student *not* attend a private or church-related school as a condition for sharing in the state's educational benefits.

The Supreme Court of the United States has repeatedly declared that parents have a constitutional right to send their children to independent schools. Yet, states demand that parents surrender this fundamental right as a condition for sharing in educational benefits.

The state's purpose in education is education—the education of children and youth. To achieve this purpose, government must provide suitable means. But government is not free to adopt any means to achieve the education of children. The means adopted to achieve the education of children is nothing more than that, the means; it can never be made the end. Hence, this means must not only be adapted to its end; it must also be consistent with the rights of parents and their children. The means may not be such as to force the surrender of constitutional rights of both parents and children.

Public educational institutions are one single means adopted by government to achieve its purpose in education—the education of children and youth. But these institutions cannot legally be the exclusive single means since the Constitution prohibits enforced conformity to the educational philosophy of state schools. The Constitution, furthermore, guarantees freedom of choice in education. Therefore, there must be other means, besides state-controlled educational institutions, which government must adopt to achieve the education of children and youth. Such means include the certificate method, tax credit, tax deduction, direct subsidization of schools, and the allocation of a part of the taxpayer's taxes to the school of his choice.

The United States is virtually the only Western democracy that has not adopted such other means to enable it to achieve, more or less equitably, the education of its children in conformity with principles of freedom of mind and freedom of religion.[10] Largely because of historical factors, we continue to demand the surrender of a constitutional right, that is, freedom of mind and freedom of religion, as a condition for sharing in the state's educational benefits.

This condition is, in effect, a compulsion to conformity to the philosophical and theological orientation of state educational institutions. All such compulsion to conformity, though it is exerted through economic pressures, is unconstitutional. The alternative to conformity is the deprivation of educational benefits. Educational subsidies are denied. Parents and students are forced to make up the denied subsidy out of their own pockets. "If taking money away from people under the taxing power may violate the first and fourteenth amendments when it tends to stifle their freedom of expression," [11] argues Alanson Willcox, "it seems plain that refusing to give them money [or welfare benefits], when the refusal is so conditioned as to tend in the same direction, may be open to the same constitutional challenge." [12]

A denial of welfare benefits to a person because of a particular action he has taken is just as restrictive and repressive as a tax burden imposed on the performance of the action itself. Consequently, state denial of benefits because of the exercise of a constitutional right merits the same condemnation, under the Constitution, as a state tax imposed on the exercise of a constitutional right. "If a tax of $7 a week may be unduly restrictive of freedom of speech," reasons Alanson Willcox, "periodic payments of the magnitude of unemployment compensation or even public assistance are not, because of their smallness, incapable of exerting such pressures as to call these amendments into play." [13] By the same token, the denial of important and costly educational benefits is capable of exerting such pressures against freedom of mind and freedom of religion as to call these amendments into play.

The denial of these benefits, operating as a restrictive economic compulsion to conformity, violates the constitutional right of parents to send their children to the school of their choice; it violates the conscience of parents who are forced by the imposed condition to send their children to government schools contrary to their religious beliefs. Yet, freedom of choice in education, based on freedom of mind and freedom of religion, is the most fundamental of all constitutional rights.

In the *Prince* case of 1944 the Supreme Court of the United

States reaffirmed the fundamental doctrine of parental right in education when it asserted the principle of "the parents' authority to provide religious with secular schooling, and the child's right to receive it, as against the state's requirement of attendance at public schools." [14]

This constitutional doctrine upholding freedom of mind and freedom of religion was reiterated by the Court in the *Everson* case of 1947. It there stated that "this Court has said that parents may, in the discharge of their duty under state compulsory education laws, send their children to a religious rather than a public school. . . ." [15] The Court was here referring to the *Pierce* or Oregon school case [16] of 1925 where it held unconstitutional a law giving the state totalitarian control over the education of all children.

It was in the *Pierce* decision that the highest court of the nation set down the fundamental principle that the child is "not the mere creature of the state." To prepare the child for "additional obligations," said the Court, is the "right . . . and the high duty" of his parents. The Oregon law compelled attendance at public schools. This law, declared the Court, "unreasonably interferes with the liberty of parents and guardians to direct the upbringing and education of children under their control." [17]

The first case challenging the right of parents to direct and control the education of their children to reach the Supreme Court of the United States was *Meyer* v. *Nebraska* in 1923.[18] In its decision, the Court repeatedly refers to the prior right of parents in the education of their children. Mr. Justice McReynolds, speaking for the Court, specifically enunciates the principle of parental "right of control" of the education of their children, "the right of parents to engage" a teacher of German to instruct their children, and "the power of parents to control the education of their own." [19]

But when parents exercise this constitutional right, their

children are deprived of all public educational benefits. The several states refuse to appropriate a farthing toward their education.

In this connection it might well be recalled that the state's obligations in education are to individual children and youth; these obligations are not to a school system or to educational institutions. Consequently, every individual child and youth has a right under the equal protection guarantee of the Fourteenth Amendment to share equally in the educational benefits made available by the state—and this without being coerced to surrender freedom of mind and freedom of religion.

The denial of educational benefits to children and youth whose parents wish to send them to independent schools is economic coercion to conformity that deprives both parents and children of basic constitutional liberties. It penalizes parents and children because of their exercise of rights guaranteed by the First Amendment. The increasing deterioration of the Bill of Rights as more and more welfare benefits are denied to more and more citizens because of their convictions and beliefs should be of the greatest concern to every American. It should be of particular concern to the courts. "It is incumbent on [the courts]," wrote Mr. Willcox, "to recognize more forthrightly than most of them have yet done how effectively the conditioning of 'privileges' can erode the Bill of Rights, and to realize that the Constitution forbids abridgement of first amendment freedoms in this way as much as in any other." [20]

If this erosion is to be stopped, the courts must be more alert to recognize that "infringement of constitutional rights is nonetheless infringement because accomplished through a conditioning of a privilege." [21]

Professor Wilber G. Katz of the University of Chicago School of Law noted in an article on "The Freedom to Believe" how great is the price exacted for the exercise of religion in the choice of school.[22] He declares, with regard to church-related schools, that "we have here applied the separation principle in a way which hampers the exercise of religious freedom. In 1925, the Supreme Court held unanimously that the constitutional liberty of parents includes a right to send their children to religious schools. *But we exact a price for the exercise of this liberty.* This is the result of our policy of taxing for the support of public education alone, and of our failure to provide tax deductions or offsets for any part of tuition paid to religious schools." [23]

But liberty at a *price* is not liberty. It is the suppression of liberty. At the very time when the lofty principles of the Bill of Rights should be taking form gradually in their hearts and minds our children are being deprived of benefits because of their exercise of a constitutional right. This impairment of liberty, experienced by some of our children and observed by others, may implant in their minds a disrespect for the rights of others that can only lead to a more rapid erosion of the Bill of Rights. It is for this reason that Mr. Justice Jackson wrote in the important *Barnette* case: "That [states] are educating the young for citizenship is reason for scrupulous protection of Constitutional freedoms of the individual, if we are not to strangle the free mind at its source and teach youth to discount important principles of our government as mere platitudes." [24]

The denial of educational benefits to independent-school children is doing the very thing that the First Amendment forbids. It prohibits the free exercise of religion. Dr. Bernard Iddings Bell, Episcopalian clergyman and educator, stated this emphatically when he wrote that "as the American school system is now conducted, more and more conducted, there is no such thing as religious liberty in American education. There is liberty only to be unreligious." [25] Canon Bell further pointed out that atheists are "allowed to force atheistic-bynegation education on the children" of Americans who believe in a God-centered education.[26]

The denial of educational benefits to children who seek a God-centered education penalizes the exercise of religion and, as such, is destructive of religious liberty. And, as Mr. Justice Black remarked in the *Douds* labor case, "freedom to think is inevitably abridged when beliefs are penalized by impositions of civil disabilities." [27] Children who are denied all state educational benefits because of their religious belief certainly suffer civil disabilities. Their freedom to think and their freedom to believe, guaranteed by the First Amendment, are abridged.

Dr. Bell, applying the principles of the First Amendment to religious freedom in education, declared that if our public schools have to be officially nonreligious, "then the only decent thing is to permit religious groups to run their own schools, which of course we now do, and to give them tax money to run them with, which we do not." [28]

This distinguished educator quotes from the encyclical of Pius XI on "The Education of Christian Youth" (1929): "Let no one say that in a nation where there are different religious beliefs, it is impossible to have public instruction otherwise than by neutral or mixed schools. In such a case it becomes the duty of the State, indeed it is the easier and more reasonable method of procedure, to leave free scope to the initiative of the Church and the family, while giving them such assistance as justice demands." Commenting on this statement of Pius XI, Dr. Bell remarked: "I am not a Roman Catholic, but I do not see how this statement can be refuted except by an appeal to prejudice. What the Pope here says applies to all sorts of private schools. The State has the right, the duty, to see to it that they are pedagogically up to standard; if they are, they should be supported on the same per capita basis as those run by the State itself." [29]

The certificate or tax credit plan enables government to fulfill its educational obligations to each child and youth consistent with constitutional principles and guarantees. The intellectual integrity and religious belief of the child and his parents are respected. The freedom of thought and freedom of religion of the individual person are given their proper rank in the hierarchy of our constitutional values. "The cardinal article of faith of our civilization is the inviolate character of the individual," remarked Mr. Justice Frankfurter. "A man can be regarded as an individual and not as a function of the state," he continued, "only if he is protected to the largest possible extent in his thoughts and in his beliefs as the citadel of his person." [30] The certificate or tax credit plan protects the integrity of the individual person in his thoughts and in his beliefs against coercive conformity to the philosophical and theological orientation of a state school system.

Enforced conformity in education stultifies democracy because it is intolerant of ideas and diversity. In an article "The Black Silence of Fear," Mr. Justice Douglas identified "the critical danger" of America—"that we will so limit or narrow the range of permissible discussion and permissible thought that we will become victims of the orthodox school." [31] We are already "victims of the orthodox school." Our children are already forced to conform to the established philosophical and theological orthodoxy of our state schools. "Our real power," Justice Douglas observes, "is our spiritual strength, and that spiritual strength stems from our civil liberties. If we are true to our traditions, if we are tolerant of a whole market place of ideas, we will always be strong. Our weakness grows when we become intolerant of opposing ideas, depart from our standards of civil liberties, and borrow the policeman's philosophy from the enemy we detest." [32]

If we are "tolerant of a whole market place of ideas," we must be tolerant of a diversity of schools; and if we are tolerant of a diversity of schools, we may not penalize students who refuse to conform to state educational philosophy and insist on pursuing their own ideas and convictions in the school of their choice. If because of our intolerance of opposing ideas we deprive millions of our children and youth of equal educational opportunities, we are indeed losing "our real power," our "spiritual strength" which "stems from our civil liberties."

The certificate or tax credit plan ensures the individual freedom and the diversity which are essential for the preservation of democracy. Democracy, if it is to flourish, must rest on individuals who are free to exercise their rights and responsibilities as *individuals*. When democracy begins to think in terms of the *masses*, the individual will soon be lost sight of, and the masses will be forced to conform, to "groupthink." The Supreme Court, rejecting the philosophy of enforced conformism and state absolutism that prevailed in the *Gobitis* case of three years earlier, declared in the *Barnette* case: "We apply the limitations of the Constitution with no fear that freedom to be intellectually and spiritually diverse or even contrary will disintegrate the social organization. . . . We can have intellectual individualism and the rich cultural diversities that we owe to exceptional minds only at the price of occasional eccentricity and abnormal attitudes." [33]

When democracy begins to think in terms of the *masses*, the right of the individual to differ shall have been lost—and with it freedom and true democracy. Enforced conformity is incompatible with the principles of the Bill of Rights. The freedom to differ is the freedom to be an individual. And, furthermore, the "freedom to differ," said the Court in the *Barnette* flag-salute case, "is not limited to things that do not matter much. That would be a mere shadow of freedom. The test of its substance is the right to differ as to things that touch the heart of the existing order." [34]

But the "freedom to differ" in the choice of education not

only does not touch or challenge "the heart of the existing order"; it is essential to that diversity and freedom of mind which gave birth to and preserves the democratic way of life.

John Stuart Mill, who like John Milton wrote most eloquently on liberty, was adamantly opposed to every form of enforced conformity. He wrote in defense of individuality and diversity, both made possible by liberty. "In championing liberty," wrote Professor William Ebenstein, "Mill has a broad goal in mind: the 'Greek ideal of self-development.' . . . Different persons should be permitted to lead different lives; and the plea for *variety* in *On Liberty* is as strong as that for *freedom*." [35] Mill rejected the idea that the development of popular self-government inevitably encompasses liberty. Like De Tocqueville he was apprehensive about the status of liberty in a democratic society. The social tyranny of a society of equals is all embracing, "penetrating much more deeply into the details of life, and enslaving the soul itself." [36] For this reason, as Ebenstein observed, "protection against political tyranny is therefore not enough; it must be supplemented by protection against the tyranny of prevailing opinion and feeling." [37] The rights and liberties of the individual must be secured by constitutional guarantees, but, no less important, society must protect the individual against the enforced imposition of ideas considered orthodox by the prevailing mood. "Mill makes the point," says Ebenstein, "that the natural disposition of man is to impose his views, as ruler or fellow citizen, on others, and that want of power is often the cause of toleration of dissent." [38]

It is for this reason, as we have seen, that Mill rejected political control of education.

Dr. Bell, ninety years later, is in complete agreement with Mill. "It is now clearly high time," he writes, "that we realize that academic freedom, freedom to seek after the truth, is threatened by no other source as it is by organized secular government." State control of education, he points out, is "never in the interest of freedom." [39] Educator Canon Bell, fully cognizant of the importance of autonomous associations in the preservation of liberty, points to the Church as a defense of freedom in education and a curb against "the State's expanding coercion." But the Church's "influence for freedom in education has grown less and less," he observes. "More and more the State has become all-controlling, directly so over the public schools and public universities—indirectly and by heavily subsidized competition over those universities and schools, religious and not so religious, which operate independently." [40]

The role of independent associations and of the Church in the defense of freedom of mind and spirit is of vital importance. "In education today, whatever may have been the case in times past, it is not the Church which threatens educational liberty, freedom of thought. On the contrary, the Church is often almost their only champion. It is the State which is the enemy of that academic freedom which, as Nicholas Murray Butler rightly said, is education's 'instrument for knowing the changing world, for aiding the changing world, for shaping the changing world,' " writes Dr. Bell.[41]

Canon Bell's injunction, given to mid-twentieth century Americans, is in defense of freedom in education. "At all costs," he warns, "state control of education must be reduced, not strengthened, if we are to have a free society competently led toward human ends." [42]

In order to avoid a monolithic government-dominated educational system, Mill, the exponent of liberty, made a concrete proposal. His proposal is substantially the certificate method. "An education established and controlled by the State should only exist, if it exist at all," he wrote, "as one among many competing experiments, carried on for the purpose of example and stimulus, to keep the others up to a certain standard of excellence." He proposed a plan in which the state would leave the choice "to parents to obtain the education where and how they pleased, and content itself with helping to pay the school fees of the poorer classes of children, and defraying the entire school expenses of those who have no one else to pay for them." [43] Applying Mill's plan to modern mass education at high costs, it would provide government educational subsidies for virtually all children and students in the schools of their choice.

Mill was so emphatically opposed to exclusive state control of education because he feared that liberty would be eroded and finally suppressed unless there was "diversity of education." "That the whole or any large part of the education of the people should be in State hands," he declared, "I go as far as any one in deprecating. All that has been said of the importance of individuality of character, and diversity in opinions and modes of conduct, involves, as of the same unspeakable importance, diversity of education." [44]

Mill's contention that complete state control of education "establishes a despotism over the mind" [45] is based on the fundamental fact that every educational institution, whether state or independent, is both philosophically and theologically oriented. The mere inculcation of facts does not of itself establish a despotism over the mind. It is the philosophical and theological orientation of these facts that enables the state through its enforced conformity to public education to "mold" the student in accordance with the "beliefs" of the dominant power in the government.

Since every educational institution is philosophically and theologically oriented, the United States Supreme Court's concluding statement in the *Barnette* opinion has particular relevance regarding the question of freedom of mind and freedom of religion in education. "If there is any fixed star in our constitutional constellation," observed the Court, "it is that no official, high or petty, can prescribe what shall be orthodox in politics, nationalism, religion, or other matters of opinion or force citizens to confess by word or act their faith therein." [46]

Since no official can prescribe what shall be "orthodox" in education, every child and student attending the school of his choice is entitled to equal educational benefits. To deny this is to assert that the state can determine what shall be "orthodox" in the field of thought and belief. And if so, non-conformists are denied educational subsidies. But this is in direct conflict with freedom of mind and freedom of religion; it is in conflict with the principle laid down by Mr. Justice Alexander of Mississippi when he declared: "The state is under duty to ignore the child's creed, but not its need. It cannot control what one child may think, but it can and must do all it can to teach the child how to think." [47]

If freedom is to endure, the state must, in the words of Mr. Justice Jackson, "let men's minds alone." When the state conditions its educational benefits on enforced conformity to state educational philosophy, it is not letting men's minds alone. It is intruding its secular arm into the mind of the student and demanding the right to orient truth as the condition for sharing in educational benefits. This violates the integrity of the human person. It subverts democracy. "Our Constitution relies on our electorate's complete ideological freedom to nourish independent and responsible intelligence and preserve our democracy from that submissiveness, timidity and herd-mindedness of the masses which would foster a tyranny of mediocrity," [48] said Justice Jackson. He emphasizes an important fact, the fact that "the priceless heritage of our society is the unrestricted constitutional right of each member to think as he will. Thought control is a copyright of totalitarianism, and we have no claim to it." [49]

Enforced conformity is the distinguishing characteristic of

the totalitarian state; freedom of mind and spirit is the distinguishing characteristic of the free democracy. In Justice Jackson's words: "If any single characteristic distinguishes our democracy from Communism it is our recognition of the individual as a personality rather than as a soulless part in the jigsaw puzzle that is the collectivist state." [50] Setting down his convictions regarding the importance of the individual person's freedom of mind and freedom of religion, the Justice observes that "our Constitution excludes both general and local governments from the realm of opinions and ideas, beliefs and doubts, heresy and orthodoxy, political, religious or scientific." [51] On the basis of this conviction, he concludes in the words of Justice Holmes that "if there is any principle of the Constitution that more imperatively calls for attachment than any other it is the principle of free thought—not free thought for those who agree with us but freedom for the thought that we hate." [52]

Perhaps the greatest defense of freedom of mind and spirit ever made was made by Justice Stone in the *Gobitis* case.[53] His was a dissenting opinion in an 8-1 decision. But his defense of freedom prevailed in the Court, nevertheless, three years later in the *Barnette* decision. Justice Stone maintained that freedom of mind and spirit stand highest in the hierarchy of our constitutional values and that these freedoms—not a coerced national unity—are the basis of national unity and strength. For this reason government school officials may not, he argued, force Jehovah's Witness children to salute the flag —to them an act of religion—as a condition of receiving the benefits of public education. He sharply rejected the proposition "that government may, as a supposed educational measure and as a means of disciplining the young, compel public affirmations which violate their religious conscience." [54] Compulsory conformity through public affirmations in conflict with conscience subverts freedom of mind and spirit.

"The guaranties of civil liberty are but guaranties of free-dom of the human mind and spirit and of reasonable freedom and opportunity to express them," [55] posits Justice Stone. Since every educational institution, as philosophically and theologically oriented, orients truth in a particular way, de-pending on its orientation, the compelled affirmation of such an orientation in the enforced attendance at state schools violates freedom of mind and spirit. "The very essence of the liberty which [the guaranties of civil liberty] guarantee," rea-sons Justice Stone, "is the freedom of the individual from compulsion as to what he shall think and what he shall say, at least where the compulsion is to bear false witness to his religion." [56] If it is assumed that years of education have an influence on the human mind, and if the "covert assumptions concerning the two basic factors with which [educational institutions] have to deal—truth and man—have been non-religious," [57] in Henry P. Van Dusen's words, is not the stu-dent who is compelled to attend a state institution as a condition for receiving educational benefits compelled "as to what he shall think," is he not compelled "to bear false witness to his religion" which would orient all particular truths to Ultimate Truth? The answer is found in the *Gobitis* dissent. "If these guarantees are to have any meaning they must, I think, be deemed to withhold from the state any authority to compel belief or the expression of it where that expression violates religious convictions. . . ." [58] The state has no authority to compel the affirmation of the philosophical and theological orientation of state educational institutions involved in the total process of education since such an affirmation "violates religious convictions."

If "legislative efforts to secure conformity of belief and opinion by a compulsory affirmation of the desired belief" [59] involved in the enforced flag salute are to be struck down (as they were in the *Barnette* case) as violations of freedom

of mind and spirit, should not, a fortiori, legislative efforts to
secure conformity to the philosophical and theological orientation of public educational institutions be struck down? The
answer may well be found in the measure of our dedication to
the Bill of Rights. "The Constitution," declared Mr. Justice
Stone, "is an expression of faith and a command that freedom
of mind and spirit must be preserved, which government must
obey, if it is to adhere to that justice and moderation without
which no free government can exist." [60]

Legislation that conditions educational benefits on the surrender of freedom of mind and spirit not only raises a constitutional question, but also calls into question the future of
democratic society. The issue is not simply one involving the
equal rights of children and students; the issue is one involving the essential nature of a society based on the dignity and
worth, the freedom of the human mind and spirit. This point
was eloquently made (and with religious flavor but not in a
religious liberty case) by Mr. Justice Frankfurter: "When
legislation touches freedom of thought and freedom of speech,
such a tendency is a formidable enemy of the free spirit. . . .
A persistent, positive translation of the liberating faith into
the feelings and thoughts and actions of men and women is
the real protection against attempts to strait-jacket the human
mind. . . . Without open minds there can be no open society.
And if society be not open the spirit of man is mutilated and
becomes enslaved." [61]

When the liberties of the individual consistently do not
prevail against the powers of government, the democratic
majority is, slowly, destroying individuality and diversity and
enforcing uniformity and conformity until there remains,
what Alexis De Tocqueville feared for democracy, only "a
flock of timid and industrious animals." [62] There will then be
only fixed attitudes and determined thought. "De Tocqueville saw—and his profound insight is still not fully grasped

and acted upon in democratic societies," observed Professor Ebenstein, "that the threat to liberty is potentially more real and menacing in a democracy than in a monarchy or an aristocracy: 'The authority of a king is purely physical, and it controls the actions of the subject without subduing his private will; but the majority possesses a power which is physical and moral at the same time; it acts upon the will as well as upon the actions of men, and it represses not only all contest, but all controversy.' " [63]

Our other-directed, socially adjusted, group-think society has proceeded a long way in subduing the private will and bringing the actions of men into conformity with the majority mood or majority will. Those who differ are not engaged in controversy but are denounced as un-American and undemocratic. They are not adjusted to the mass; they are nonconformists. They are, consequently, degraded to the level of second-class citizens. Democratic despotism, as opposed to the classical forms, "would," De Tocqueville saw, "be more extensive and more mild; it would degrade men without tormenting them." [64]

De Tocqueville had a profound understanding of the power of public opinion in democratic society. Public opinion, he saw, has the power to ostracize, shun, spurn, and destroy the political career of individuals of unorthodox and nonconformist views. "Nothing disturbed Tocqueville more in his study of democracy," observed Ebenstein, "than the 'quiet and gentle' kind of terror and intimidation that does not destroy, but prevents, existence; that does not tyrannize, but compresses, enervates, extinguishes, and stupefies people 'till each nation is reduced to be nothing better than a flock of timid and industrious animals, of which the government is the shepherd.' " [65]

How can the tyranny of the majority in democracy, feared by both De Tocqueville and Mill as all but inevitable, be resisted? This is a major domestic problem that confronts democratic America today.

Enforced conformity through majority action—this is the persistent evil that De Tocqueville feared for America. Today, more and more pressure is being exerted to force all to conform to the "accepted" way of doing things. That is "accepted" which is the pattern established by the prevailing mood. Individuals are denounced because their religious beliefs do not conform; parents are denounced because they are nonconformists in their choice of school; philosophers are denounced because they accept absolute moral principles; educators are denounced because they believe the purpose of education is to educate; moral idealists are denounced because they uphold moral standards which transcend the common morality of the masses; religious leaders are denounced because they are nonconformists in their insistence upon the importance of God in the education of the young.

Americans are being more and more forced to conform in thought and belief. Sometimes this is accomplished through social pressure; sometimes through the instrumentality of state pressure as when children and students who will not conform to state educational policy are deprived of all state educational benefits. Conformity to the philosophical and theological orientation of state educational institutions is the prerequisite condition for sharing in educational funds. Economic pressure is used to strait-jacket the thinking and belief of our children.

These burdens and penalties imposed on dissenters and nonconformists tend, by design or otherwise, to exterminate the dissenters. School children and youth are coerced to conform to the policies imposed by the controlling majority. This enables the controlling factor to achieve that "compulsory unification of opinion" which Mr. Justice Jackson remarked "achieves only the unanimity of the graveyard." [66]

This denial of liberty, this enforced conformity, is not just a matter of depriving a minority of individual citizens of their constitutional freedoms and equal rights. It is more than that. The whole moral fiber of our constitutional democracy depends on a fair respect by courts and legislatures alike for the liberties and rights of all Americans, regardless of race, color, or religious affiliation. If government does not rise to this level, then democracy fails. In his defense of democracy and freedom in the *Gobitis* dissent, Mr. Justice Stone, it may be recalled, set forth this fundamental truth in no uncertain terms. "The Constitution expresses more than the conviction of the people that democratic *processes* must be preserved at all costs," he wrote. "It is also an expression of faith and a command that *freedom* of *mind* and *spirit* must be preserved, which government must obey, if it is to adhere to that justice and moderation without which no free government can exist." [67]

These principles of individual freedom underlie the concluding paragraphs of the summary of the Rockefeller Brothers Fund report on "The Pursuit of Excellence: Education and the Future of America." It declares that the students' "education is based upon the notion of the dignity and worth of the individual because those values are rooted in our religious and philosophical heritage." Taking cognizance of the consequent rights and freedom of the individual student, the report states that "we would not wish to impose upon students a rigidly defined set of values. Each student is free to vary the nature of his commitment. But this freedom must be understood in its true light. We believe that the individual should be free and morally responsible: the two are inseparable. The fact that we tolerate differing values must not be confused with moral neutrality. Such tolerance must be built upon a base of moral commitment; otherwise it degenerates into a flaccid indifference, purged of all belief and devotion." [68]

There can be no enforced conformity. The student must be free in his commitment; his personal integrity must be respected. "In short," concludes the Rockefeller Brothers Fund report, "we wish to allow wide latitude in the choice of values but we must assume that education is a process that should be infused with meaning and purpose; that everyone will have deeply held beliefs; that every young American will wish to serve the values which have nurtured him and made possible his education and his freedom as an individual." [69]

# 4

# Gifted Children
# and Freedom of Choice

*The certificate or tax credit plan would enable parents of gifted children to select high-quality schools.*

The American school system has adopted many programs to provide for nontypical children. There are programs for the deaf, the blind, the mentally retarded, and so forth. Special attention given to nontypical children achieves the lofty purpose of enabling them to take their place as useful citizens in American society.

But there has been too little organized effort to provide for the proper development of exceptionally gifted children. Dr. M. M. Boring, consultant to President Eisenhower's Committee on Scientists and Engineers, remarked that "we will do all sorts of things for the unfortunates—the lower group—but we don't do a thing for the outstanding kids with high intelligence." [1]

Programs of studies for outstanding boys and girls have been repeatedly killed as undemocratic. Democracy has come to mean conformity to undistinguishable mediocrity. Conformity demands that there be no recognition of exceptional talents—hence, all rivalry is rejected from the classroom. "Ours should be a 'democratic education' indeed—as our rhetorical pedagogues repeatedly assert," says Canon Bernard

Iddings Bell. "But the critics [of 'education'] are no longer exorcised by the glib use of that magic phrase. 'Democratic education'—splendid!—but the beauty of the adjective does not conceal the vacuity of the noun. Let whatever we have be 'democratic'—but let us be sure it is also *education*." [2]

Frequently, fuzzy-minded notions of equality and democracy are carried to the extent of outlawing the grading system in our schools. The only grade given is that of conformity or nonconformity: the child is "adjusted" or "not adjusted." Adjusted or not adjusted to what? To other children considered as a *mass*.

The reason for this trend is perhaps not difficult to discover. Dr. Arnold O. Beckman, educator and manufacturer, declared that "the broad socialistic movement, which has engulfed our country as well as other countries, which tends to destroy competition, eliminate free enterprise and destroy individual initiative, shows up in our school system in several ways. One is the attempt to do away with a competitive grading system in our public schools. . . . Some schools even went so far as to attempt to grade pupils not on their performance in an absolute sense but upon their performance in relation to their estimated ability, as measured by an I.Q. test or some other means. On the basis of this standard, a moron who handed in all of his home work—even though it was worthless—would receive a higher grade than a brilliant student who was somewhat careless in turning in his papers." [3]

Senator Ralph Flanders told a congressional committee that the public school of Springfield, Vermont, his home, adopted a policy stating "that examinations shall be student-based and not subject-based. In other words," he clarified, "it is of no great importance whether a child really understands the mathematics so long as he is working hard at it. If so, he gets a good grade. But as to whether he has achieved a satisfactory degree of proficiency is not of any particular interest to the school." [4]

This method, so destructive of individual initiative, is not easily surrendered by the educationists, even when subjected to attack by parents. Dr. Beckman writes that "in some school districts where indignant parents have demanded that grades be re-established, the attempt is made to minimize the significance of grades denoting proficiency, by having several other grades for each course. In arithmetic, for example, there are grades which purportedly measure such things as 'responsibility and self-direction, and relationship with others.' " [5] The idea of conformity or adjustment to the mass, without any significant differentiating quality points, is retained.

This grading system is but indicative of an attitude that shows little interest in developing the capabilities of our boys and girls to their highest levels. What inspiration does a girl with an intelligence quotient of 130 get out of being told that she is well "adjusted"? Or what challenge does a boy with an I.Q. of 135 get out of being told that he is "not adjusted"? His maladjustment may well be the result of sheer boredom with classes and subjects that hold absolutely no interest for him.

Speaking of the high mortality rate among intellectually able young people, Dr. Arthur Bestor, University of Illinois, says that "American public schools give totally inadequate recognition to intellectual achievement. No wonder the incentive to work hard at difficult subjects is so much weaker here than in other countries." [6] The failure of our schools to give adequate "recognition to intellectual achievement" is consequent upon the fact that the performance of our schools, determined to a considerable degree by their attitude toward things intellectual, is itself not subject to the challenge of competitive schools. As a result the competitive incentive to produce at the highest level of excellence in difficult subjects is lacking in the schools. With this attitude prevailing in the schools, it is not difficult to understand why the pupils lack "the incentive to work hard at difficult subjects."

"There's another reason why such an alarming percentage of our ablest young men and women feel no desire to complete their education," writes Professor Bestor. "Their intellectual interest and intellectual curiosity have been deadened because they have been held back to the level of the mediocre student so long that they have become completely bored. A 'soft' educational system has put their brains to sleep." [7]

When children of every mental age are thrown together in the same class, the teacher invariably gives major attention to the problems of the slow learner and little attention to the gifted children. In such a classroom situation, talented children will not be encouraged, challenged, and inspired to do their best—even supposing the teacher is competent and willing and the atmosphere of the school is not anti-intellectual. They will not only not advance as rapidly as possible, but there is every danger that they will become problem children.

"The facts discovered by educational psychology about individual differences in rates and levels of learning are incontestable," writes Monsignor Thomas J. Quigley, former superintendent of schools and member of the Federal Education Commission in 1955. "These should have led us to a re-organization of our educational system into different kinds of schools or at least different kinds of curricula." [8]

The American youngster is by nature a competitor. He loves a challenge. The tougher the challenge, the greater the effort he will put forth to conquer. He meets the competitive challenge with enthusiasm, with determination, with a real desire to excel and to win. But when, on the other hand, there is no competition and rivalry, when there is no direction, challenge, or inspiration from his teacher, the American youngster, surrounded by many captivating distractions, all too often loses interest in studies, develops habits of laziness, mental sloppiness and, too frequently, the characteristics of the typical problem child.

In view of this situation, Monsignor Quigley concludes that "our gifted pupils simply cannot be properly nor thoroughly educated in our present-day high school (nor even elementary school). It is the height of the ridiculous to expect a teacher in a single classroom of 50 pupils to keep the genius and the moron and everyone between working, each at his own best rate and level." [9] This problem must be met realistically. The fact that some children are considerably more talented than others must be recognized in our school organization. "If we need special schools for the retarded," writes the former superintendent, "we need special schools for the gifted; schools for our future scientists, mathematicians, engineers, doctors, lawyers, philosophers, and theologians; schools where the brilliant survive, where the only test of success is mastery of the traditional subject-matter fields." [10]

But is not such a recognition of talent undemocratic? Does it not establish an intellectual élite? Is this not completely at variance with the "life adjustment" philosophy of education? "An educational system that refuses to single out for high and exceptional honors those who demonstrate in fair competition their brilliance and their willingness to work," writes Arthur Bestor, "is not a democratic school system at all. It is simply an anti-intellectual school system." [11]

The Illinois history professor, a critic of "life adjustment" education, commenting on the January 2, 1958, report of the Educational Policies Commission of the National Educational Association, said: "In particular, the report expresses nothing but hostility for 'rigorous' programs of study for able students —exactly the kind that students of this caliber require—because in the past 'such curricula were used to weed out the less able pupils and relegate them to inferior schools, thereby producing both an elite and a mass of followers.' " Pointedly, the professor remarked: "Now I don't want inferior schools for anybody. But if you lower the standards of the schools for fear of giving too good an education to bright students, then you are deliberately *creating* inferior schools, and—most suicidal of all—forcing the best talent of the nation to go to waste in them." [12]

If we must "lower the standards of the schools for fear of giving too good an education to bright students," it becomes impossible to meet the standards of the Russian "high school" and to match its product. In effect, we concede defeat to the USSR in the contest of scientific and intellectual achievement by deliberately refusing to meet the Soviet challenge in the classroom where the battle of the future is being waged. President Eisenhower, in his first broadcast after the launching of the Soviet satellites, called the nation's attention to the quality of the education received by children in the Soviet Union. He said: "Remember that, when a Russian graduates from high school, he has had five years of physics, fours years of chemistry, one year of astronomy, five years of biology, ten years of mathematics through trigonometry, and five years of a foreign language." [13]

The educationists' fear of creating an intellectual "élite" may make it extremely difficult to change radically the quality of American high school education described by Marion B. Folsom, Secretary of Health, Education, and Welfare. In a memorandum of December 30, 1957, he reported: "Studies indicate, for example, that only 1 out of 3 high school graduates [in the United States] has had a year of chemistry, only 1 out of 4 has taken a year of physics, and only 1 out of 3 has had more than one year of algebra." [14] Furthermore, only 1 out of 8 of our high school students get either trigonometry or solid geometry.[15] State legislatures under the influence of powerful pressure groups have a considerable voice in determining the intellectual or anti-intellectual orientation of our government schools. In 1957 fourteen states required not a single course in science or mathematics for a high school diploma. And "while 27 states maintain special supervisors for physical education, and all 48 have supervisors for home economics, agriculture and 'distributive trades,' only two states employ a mathematics supervisor, and only six have supervisors for science," reported *Time* magazine.[16]

If this is a discouraging picture, we can take even less consolation in our schools' productivity in the area of the foreign languages. Not 15 per cent of all United States high school students take even a single foreign language. Moreover, 50 per cent of our high schools do not offer their students the opportunity to take a foreign language. If we compare our foreign-language performance with the Russian performance, it is extremely interesting to note that while only ten out of 25,000 United States high schools offer Russian, 40 per cent of all Russian high school students study English. In this field, said Secretary Marion Folsom, "we find ourselves the most backward major nation in the world." [17]

There is no reason to believe that American youth are less talented and potentially less interested in studies than are Russian children. There is no reason to believe that American youngsters, if given the opportunity and if properly inspired and challenged, would not do as well in the study of algebra, geometry, trigonometry, physics, and chemistry as do the youngsters in the schools of the Soviet Union. There is no reason to believe that American youngsters, if given the opportunity and if properly inspired and challenged, would not do as well in the study of languages, literature, the social sciences, and the arts as do the youngsters in the schools of the Soviet.

It is a generally admitted fact that our educational system is not producing the results of the Soviet system. Professor

John Ise, University of Kansas, speaking with forty-two years of college teaching experience, sharply states the reasons why this is so. "We're trying too hard to make education painless," he declares. The Kansas professor makes the further indictment that "the public schools have, of course, never dared to do much but inoculate their pupils against thinking about important questions." [18]

Dr. Harold W. Dodds, former president of Princeton University, expresses the same conviction when he takes issue with the leveling of public school programs in favor of "easy knowledge, lax instruction, over-emphasis on extracurricular activities and other escapes." Indicating that there were numerous "striking exceptions," the Princeton president declared that "unfortunately when we come to view America's vast system of tax-supported secondary education we are, I fear, bound to admit that, with all that it has to its credit, too often it is not fulfilling its duty to cultivate the instinct to think." [19]

Why is our government secondary educational system failing in "its duty to cultivate the instinct to think"? Is it because of a lack of money? The *Wall Street Journal* says emphatically that the cure for our educational deficiencies is not money. Commenting on Mr. Folsom's proposal to attack our educational deficiencies with a billion dollars of Federal funds, the *Journal* remarks that "the saddest thing about all this is not the waste of money nor the proliferation of bureaucracy, foolish though they be. It is that having suddenly awakened to the way our educational system has wasted the Nation's bright young minds, we seem beguiled by the notion that we can put everything right by opening our pocketbooks. We of Mr. Folsom's generation have not failed our young out of miserliness and we will not repair that injustice with a billion dollars. For whatever the reason why too few students learn science or algebra or language it is not a shortage of available funds. The schools are there, built by the taxpayers. The students are there, taking something. The teachers are there, teaching something. The cure is not in money but in mind, the mind of the community, and the teachers, to have things otherwise." [20]

In the educational atmosphere described by Professor Ise and Princeton's former President Dodds, the gifted and talented boy and girl have little or no opportunity to develop to the highest level of their capacity. This is an injustice to them. It is an injustice to American society. It is an injustice to Western civilization and to human society in general.

When society makes an investment in the moral and intellectual development of a boy or girl, it has a right to expect that those who have assumed the obligation to educate will create the conditions and circumstances that will enable the pupil to develop his talents to their highest potential. Society has a right to expect that its potential leaders will not be lost because of an inept educational system.

If our educational system is failing in its duty to gifted students and to society, no one will deny that remedies should be adopted. Rear Admiral Hyman G. Rickover, Chief of the Naval Reactors Branch of the Atomic Energy Commission, both recognizes the failures of our schools and makes concrete remedial proposals. "To put it bluntly," he said, "our schools do not perform their primary purpose, which is to train the nation's brain power to the highest potential." [21]

In his proposal for achieving this primary purpose he said, "We shall not do justice to our talented youth until we seek them out at an early age—no later than 10 or 11—and educate them separately from the rest of the children. This should be done preferably in separate schools or if this is not possible in separate classes." Admiral Rickover insists, moreover, that the separate schools would be staffed by teachers, "whose qualifications place less emphasis on training in teaching methods and more on graduate study in their fields." [22]

If America and Western civilization are to survive, it is imperatively necessary that we develop the nation's brain power to its highest potential. Admiral Lewis L. Strauss, Chairman of the United States Atomic Energy Commission, said in July, 1956: "In 5 years our country's lead in the training of scientists and engineers may be wiped out. In 10 years it could be hopelessly outstripped. Unless immediate steps are taken to correct it, a situation, already dangerous, within less than a decade could become disastrous." [23] Since the launching of the Soviet satellites the admiral's apprehensions about scientific education in the United States are undoubtedly considerably greater.

The *New York Times* pointed out editorially the consequences of a lack of scientific manpower. The editor writes that "disturbing rumors are circulating that for lack of scientific manpower we are not improving guided missiles or advancing the utilization of atomic energy as rapidly as we should." In assigning reasons for this lack of brain power, the *Times* says that "our basic weakness is traceable largely to our secondary schools, which are simply not good enough when it comes to teaching science, whereas in Soviet Russia science is the principal concern of teachers in secondary schools." [24]

Dr. John R. Weir, associate professor of psychology and director of student counseling at the California Institute of Technology, directed a study entitled "Brain Power." Professor Weir's study revealed "the immensity of the waste in the development of intellectual talent in the United States. We lose half of the capable, a third of the exceptionally talented." The study continues:

The considerations most relevant to the making of a scientist or an engineer readily fall into three categories: (1) early identification, (2) encouragement, and (3) training.

1. Clearly the earlier we can identify the embryo scientist or

engineer the better. We are beginning to know a little about the psychological, emotional, and cultural experiences that are of importance in the ultimate determination of such an occupational choice. . . .

2. The second set of problems relates to the encouragement or the development, of the budding scientist or engineer. His social-class origin, his home environment, his parents' attitudes toward intellectual knowledge, the distractions of competing interests and activities, are all important determinants of motivation for continued learning.

In the elementary and high schools, the manner in which science and mathematics are taught and the enthusiasm and understanding of the teacher often have tremendous influence in awakening the spark of curiosity in young students. . . .

And finally, there is the need for the removal of financial barriers so that any qualified and deserving student—the capable as well as the outstanding—can complete his education.

3. The third set of problems may be grouped around training or education.

At the high-school level there is a serious shortage of math and science teachers; we are producing only half of what we need, and only half of those produced go into teaching. . . .[25]

All of these things can be done. And they can be done efficiently and effectively if we will but adopt the means necessary. We shall never solve the problem of identifying our potentially great students and scholars, nor shall we encourage, inspire, and develop those we do identify to their greatest potentiality by merely spending more money. There is no solution in multiplying our past mistakes. We must have the courage, the strength, the fortitude to adopt the means, consistent with constitutional principles, to provide those conditions that will enable us to inspire children, young men and women to their highest excellence on every level of education. Nothing could be more disastrous to democracy and Western civilization than our refusal to wage the war against communism on the field of battle selected by the USSR—in the classroom. The tactical decisions of war must, in this instance, be made to meet the aggressive attacks of the enemy; they must not be made on the basis of sentiment or personal prepossessions.

In 1956 the California Institute of Technology conducted a series of conferences with the executives of corporations affiliated with the institute through its industrial associates program. The purpose of these conferences was to review the problems which will confront the world during the next century. The *New York Times* in a signed article summarizes some of the findings of these conferences. The author writes:

Man is now standing at the gateway to a new flowering of civilization.

The population of the earth will multiply at least 2 or 4 times in the next 100 years. Technology can feed, clothe and shelter these people adequately and in some cases well.

There will be no shortage of minerals, meals or metals. Machine civilization will spread over the earth and it can provide for all from the most common substances: air, sea water, ordinary rock and sunlight.

Only one possible raw material shortage is foreseen—brain power. Educated men and women are needed to plan and design, to construct and operate the machine civilization that will care for the startling increase in world population expected by the year 2050.

Brain power is the key, education, government and industry must meet in a deliberate and sustained effort to sense the future and to plan for it. There is a chasm that technology must hurdle: raw materials and food already are running short just as the earth's population starts its greatest increase: from 2,600,000,000 persons today to some 6,700,000,000 persons in 100 years. Possibly more.[26]

It is a sad commentary on the good sense and wisdom of man to intimate that the heavens and earth contain a super-

abundance of raw materials to supply the needs of a rapidly
increasing population, but that, because of our refusal to
adopt the necessary means to develop the needed brain power,
our great-grandchildren will have to fight for the food necessary for survival. If "brain power is the key" to successfully
meeting the problems of the future, let us then use the means,
radical though they may seem to conformitarians, that will
inspire gifted children, young men and women to develop
their talents to their highest potential. This is no time to
applaud complacency, mediocrity, and conformism. This is
the time to take the action dictated by reason and demanded
by the Constitution. Parents must be given freedom of choice
in education.

Dr. John R. Weir, one of the Institute panelists, emphasized the importance of our developing the available brain
power to meet the scientific problems of the future. He maintained that there would be "an ever-increasing need for more
skilled manpower, for more trained scientists and engineers."
The "critical limiting factor on the world's resources," Professor Weir pointed out, "is not materials, energy, or food, but
brain power." We are already experiencing a shortage of engineers and scientists. Although there is a real lack of truly
scholarly men and women in all the fields of knowledge, yet,
as Dr. Weir says, "the big problem is the waste in the development of intellectual talent. Half the capable young men and
women are not educated, one-third of the exceptionally talented are not educated." [27]

There is reason to believe that this critical shortage of scientists and engineers would be overcome if parents enjoyed freedom of choice in education. If parents had freedom of choice,
they could and would select those schools—public or private
—that provide the inspiration and challenge needed to develop their children to their highest excellence. If parents
enjoyed this freedom of choice, they would send their children

to schools of high quality. This would, in turn, create a competitive situation that would cause to be developed a variety of schools to meet the demands of the educational market place.

The certificate or tax credit plan would bring about the development of schools of the highest excellence. Such schools would not be based on the principle described by Dr. John A. Hannah, president of Michigan State University, as a "fuzzy-minded indulgence in equality in education for the sake of equality." [28] Rather, such schools would be based on the principle described by the *Saturday Review* in a guest editorial as *"the freedom to be one's best."* [29]

"The freedom to be one's best," says the *Review*, "is the chance for the development of each person to his highest power." This notion is based on the primary postulate of the spiritual freedom of the individual from government controls and inhibitions. It assumes the freedom of the individual student to develop his capacities to their highest excellence; this in turn assumes freedom of mind and religion in the pursuit of truth.

The principle of "the freedom to be one's best" rejects the notion that democracy demands that all education must be geared to the middle of the class. The principle of mediocrity is rejected in the sports world, in the business world, in the literary world, in the professional world. Why should it be tolerated—or made inevitable—in the educational world, an area of such fundamental importance that it affects directly all other areas of human activity? Mediocrity in education cannot be justified. Mediocrity in education, however, can be explained by the fact that education on the primary and secondary levels is, for all practical purposes, nearly completely socialized. Socialization breeds mediocrity, whether in business, the professions, or education.

The notion that superior students must be cut down to the

level of the average student is not consequent upon the democratic ideal; it is consequent upon the socialistic ideal. This ideal leads, in the name of democracy, to what the *Saturday Review* calls "the middle-muddle. Courses are geared to the middle of the class. The good student is unchallenged, bored. The loafer receives his passing grade. And the lack of an outstanding course for the outstanding student, the lack of a standard which a boy or girl must meet, passes for democracy." [30]

The principle of "the freedom to be one's best" demands that we provide for our children the most demanding, the most challenging curriculum that is within their capabilities. Such a curriculum, together with the freedom of choice ensured by the certificate or tax credit plan would, in all probability, give us scholars not only equal in number and quality with the Soviet Union. It would, under the inspiration of liberty and free competitive enterprise, give us scholars superior in both number and quality. To deny this is to have lost confidence in the value of true liberty and free competitive enterprise.

This freedom of choice and "freedom to be one's best" means education for inequality. But this is the meaning of true education, so aptly described by Felix Schelling: "True education makes for inequality; the inequality of individuality, the inequality of success; the glorious inequality of talent, of genius; for inequality, not mediocrity, individual superiority, not standardization, is the measure of the progress of the world." [31]

"Education of this kind," says President Hannah, "recognizes first of all that there is a great deal of difference in individuals—in their personalities, their intelligence quotients, in their special aptitudes, in their attitudes, in their motivations. It recognizes that true intelligence is a quality to be sought after more diligently than we seek uranium, and to be cher-

ished far more closely than any of the more flamboyant qualities to which we are prone to lavish our admiration and our
material rewards. Most important, it recognizes the failure to
develop such intelligence to its fullest extent and greatest
social usefulness as a folly this nation cannot afford." [32]

This folly must be ended forthwith. A long step can be
taken in the direction of putting an end to it by enabling
parents to send their gifted children to schools best equipped
to develop their talents to their highest potential. The certificate or tax credit plan would enable parents to send their
children to schools, whether government or independent, that
have demonstrated their excellence through the quality of
their graduates.

"We need quality," declares the Rockefeller Brothers Fund
report, "and we need it in considerable quantity." We need
quality not merely for survival; we need it to preserve and
vitalize our democratic institutions. "Every democracy must
encourage high individual performance," observes the report.
"If it does not then it closes itself off from the mainsprings
of its dynamism and talent and imagination, and the traditional democratic invitation to the individual to realize his
full potentialities becomes meaningless." Excellence, moreover, is not beyond the reach of present-day America. "The
truth is," the Rockefeller panel maintains, "that never in our
history have we been in a better position to commit ourselves
wholeheartedly to the pursuit of excellence." [33]

# Freedom to Choose a
# God-Centered Education

*The certificate or tax credit plan enables parents to secure for their children a God-centered education.*

The freedom of choice made possible by the certificate or tax credit plan enables parents and students to select schools which teach the eternal values to which the Founding Fathers of our nation adhered. These are the values which underlie the educational ideals set forth in the Northwest Ordinance which was readopted by the First Congress of the United States: "*Religion, morality,* and knowledge being necessary to good government and the happiness of mankind, schools and the means of education shall forever be encouraged." [1] To the Founding Fathers of our American democracy, the prime purpose of education and schools was to teach "religion" and "morality" and to impart "knowledge" because these are essential both to the individual and to civil society.

The religious and moral values that inspired the members of the First Congress had previously inspired the signers of the Declaration of Independence. The signers of the Declaration, giving full recognition to the transcendent and essential importance of God in a free society, declared "that all men are created equal, that they are endowed by their Creator with certain unalienable Rights, that among these are Life, Liberty, and the Pursuit of Happiness." [2] Further, these are

78

the values that moved President Washington to emphasize in his Farewell Address: "Of all the dispositions and habits which lead to political prosperity, *religion* and *morality* are indispensable supports. In vain would that man claim the tribute of patriotism who should labor to subvert these great pillars of human happiness—these firmest props of the duties of men and citizens." [3] American civilization today demonstrates President Washington's wisdom. With the subversion of the pillars of religion and morality in American society, there have arisen domestic, social, and political problems which have become all but insoluble because "these firmest props of the duties of men and citizens" have been subverted. And their subversion has brought about the weakening and disintegration of our democratic values.

"And let us with caution indulge the supposition," warned Washington, "that morality can be maintained without religion. Whatever may be conceded to the influence of refined education on minds of peculiar structure, reason and experience both forbid us to expect that national morality can prevail in exclusion of religious principle." [4] Again, it must be said that history has proved the wisdom of the First President of the United States. Court and police records seem to provide irrefutable proof that once religion (in the positive sense in which Washington understood the term) has been plucked from the heart of a free nation and the majority of its people there remain no foundation stones upon which to build the moral structures of life. With the eradication of religion, the moral life of a people rapidly deteriorates.

These values of our Founding Fathers are in sharp contrast to "some of the most influential tenets" which, maintains the *Saturday Review* in a guest editorial by Seymour St. John, have characterized (not universally, we trust) "teacher education over the past fifty years: *there is no eternal truth; there is no absolute moral law; there is no God.* Yet all of history has taught us," continues the *Review*, "that the denial of these ultimates, the placement of man or state at the core of the universe, results in a paralyzing mass selfishness; and the first signs of it are already frighteningly evident." [5]

This philosophy makes the state the source of all our rights and liberties. Our most treasured freedoms become mere concessions of the state. But if our liberties are mere concessions of the state, the state has the right and power to take them away. This doctrine does, in fact, give the state total power— it is the philosophy of the absolute state.

It may come as a shock to realize how far we have retreated from the thought and philosophy that gave birth to and nurtured our American democracy. This retreat from a philosophy of freedom to a philosophy of the absolute state is clearly indicated by contrasting the tenets of teacher education with the ethical and theological theses and propositions that students in our colonial colleges publicly defended in a demonstration of intellectual achievement.

Harvard students, both theological and secular, were prepared to defend these theological theses, for example, in 1769: (1) Theology treats of the knowledge of God and of all things pertaining to eternal felicity. (2) A miracle in itself is credible. (3) There was need of divine revelation for Christianity. (4) The principles of religion are in harmony with human nature and with reason alone as a leader would never have been accepted; therefore (5) The clarity of method of the writers of today and the rightness of their sentiments in treating of natural religion arises to the greatest extent from divine revelation. [6]

The ethical theses that the Harvard student was prepared to defend publicly in 1810 included: (1) Moral precepts are deduced only from the will of God. (2) The precepts which are called the laws of nature reason unfolds to mankind. (3) The difference between good and evil, virtue and vice, set up by God is immutable; because it is founded on the nature of things. (4) The expectation of reward or punishment connected with the command of God is absolutely necessary for moral obligations. (5) God demands the actions which beget happiness; He prohibits those which bring misery. (6) It is necessary that the will of God as a criterion be the test of happiness of our actions. (7) The divine laws concern especially thought; because on them our actions depend.[7]

"The ethical theses that are available from the four colleges, Harvard, Yale, Princeton, and Brown," concludes James J. Walsh in his book *Education of the Founding Fathers of the Republic,* "are all sufficently alike to make it clear that they represent the moral philosophy teaching of the time." [8]

The philosophical principles which Jefferson wrote into the Declaration of Independence are those which are found in theses defended in the colleges of his day. Common among these is the proposition that men have inherent rights and that they have the right and the duty to defend them even at the peril of their lives. "Jefferson's formulas with regard to the equality of men, the seat of authority in the people, the right to be consulted in the levying of taxes, are all definite propositions in medieval philosophy taught at all the colonial colleges," [9] writes James Walsh.

Theses, scholastic in origin, which were reflected in the Declaration of Independence, are found among the commencement propositions defended in colonial colleges. Some of these theses are: (1) The right of kings had its original foundation from popular compact. (Princeton in 1750.) (2) Government when it is not by the voice of the people verges toward tyranny. (Brown in 1771.) (3) Absolute monarchy tends to the destruction of the happiness of the human race. (Harvard in 1765.) (4) No civil law is just unless it agrees with the principles of the natural law. (Harvard in 1778.) (5) The will of God accords perfectly with the happiness of society. (Harvard in 1778.) (6) The persuasion of the existence of God is necessary for the preservation of civil society. (Harvard in 1770.) [10]

"There is a definite similarity among the theses at all the colonial colleges," observes Dr. Walsh. "The propositions were almost identical and as a rule there are only word differences. . . . Harvard one hundred and fifty years after its first Commencement, and Yale nearly a hundred years after its initial disputation were still setting up practically the same theses for 'manful defense' as they did at the beginning." [11]

The best indication of the influence of the philosophical and theological teaching of the colonial colleges upon the minds of their students is found in the propositions of the Declaration of Independence. The propositions to which the signers of the Declaration, products for the most part of our colonial colleges, set down their names declare "that all men are created equal, that they are endowed by their Creator with certain unalienable Rights, that among these are Life, Liberty, and the Pursuit of Happiness. That to secure these rights, Governments are instituted among Men, deriving their just powers from the consent of the governed. . . ." [12]

Thomas Jefferson, graduate of William and Mary, articulated the same philosophy when he declared that "the God who gave us life gave us liberty at the same time." [13] And John Adams reflected the religious and philosophical nature of his Harvard education when he wrote: "I would ask, by what law the parliament has authority over America? By the law of God, in the Old and New Testament, it has none; . . . by the common law of England, it has none. . . ." [14] Alexander Hamilton, student at King's College, now Columbia University, was imbued with the same natural-law philosophy that motivated and guided the steady hand of our nation's first President, George Washington. Hamilton wrote: "The sacred rights of mankind are not to be rummaged for among old parchments or musty records. They are written, as with a sunbeam, in the whole volume of human nature, by the hand of Divinity Itself, and can never be erased or obscured by mortal powers." [15]

The famous Boston lawyer James Otis expresses clearly the God-centered natural-law philosophy that gave birth to our democracy and sets limits to the powers of government: "To say the parliament is absolute and arbitrary, is a contradiction. The parliament cannot make 2 and 2, 5: Omnipotency cannot do it. The supreme power in a state, is *jus dicere* only: —*jus dare*, strictly speaking, belongs alone to God. Parliaments are in all cases to *declare* what is for the good of the whole; but it is not the *declaration* of parliament that makes it so: There must be in every instance, a higher authority, viz. God. Should an act of parliament be against any of *His* natural laws, which are *immutably* true, *their* declaration would be contrary to eternal truth, equity and justice, and consequently void: and so it would be adjudged by the parliament itself, when convinced of their mistake." [16]

Finally, President Eisenhower warned us against the philosophy espoused by modern secularists in his address of February 20, 1955. He said: "Without God there could be no American form of government, nor an American way of life. Recognition of the Supreme Being is the first—the most basic—expression of Americanism. Thus the founding fathers saw it, and thus, with God's help, it will continue to be." He said, moreover, that the "founding fathers expressed in words for all to read the ideal of government based upon human dignity," and the "recognition of God as the author of individual rights." Man's fundamental rights are from God—not from the state. For, said the President, "if the state gives rights, it can—and inevitably will—take away those rights." [17]

This truth of the fundamental relation between belief in God and the foundation, operation, and preservation of democracy was reiterated by the Supreme Court in the *Zorach* case of 1952. While upholding the right of the public school child to learn about God during his schooling hours, the Court pointed out that "we are a religious people whose institutions presuppose a Supreme Being." [18]

The "institutions" of the American way of life that presuppose a Supreme Being are many. A few examples will suffice. The Bill of Rights would be as meaningless as the declaration of "Fundamental Rights of Citizens" in the Constitution of the USSR of 1936, if it were not based on the proposition that man's rights are "inalienable" because they have their source in God. Man's liberty is the liberty of the sons of God. Democracy itself is rooted in the belief that the individual person has rights, dignity, and worth; but the person possesses these qualities and rights because, as Thomas F. Woodlock wrote, "God created him to have them." [19]

Our whole legal system is based upon the proposition that there is a difference between right and wrong; but this distinction is meaningless unless there is an ultimate criterion of "rightness" which transcends man's world. In its operations our democratic form of government, functioning through its executive, legislative, and judicial branches, presupposes freedom of choice in public officials. But this use of free will in making choices for the public good presupposes a norm for judging what is good for a people. If the norm does not transcend nature, if it is not objectively right and just, then the code of the jungle prevails. Finally, constitutionalism means precisely that a higher law, the source of the individual citizen's rights and duties, places limits to the powers of government. Government does not possess total power over citizens. This higher law is the Law of God for man's temporal government.

Jefferson, one of the nation's greatest defenders of personal liberty, asked the important question: "Can the liberties of a nation be thought secure when we have removed their only firm basis, a conviction in the minds of the people that their liberties are the gift of God?" [20]

Jefferson's question cannot be easily dismissed. Nor can we ignore the implications of the answer. Conviction follows knowledge. And systematic knowledge is the product of education. Hence Jefferson's question may be rephrased: Can the liberties of our nation be secure when we fail to teach our children and youth man's relations to God and God's relations to man? The answer was clear in Jefferson's mind. His conviction that our liberties have their origin in God and his conviction that our liberties are secure only if we recognize this fact induced him, when president of the University of Virginia, to authorize the teaching of religion at the state university that he had founded.[21]

The third President of the United States, like the thirty-fourth President, was deeply convinced that the "only firm basis" of our "liberties" is God. And Jefferson, like Eisenhower, was convinced that if our liberties are mere concessions of the state the state can and inevitably will take them away. Hence there is nothing more important for the preservation of our freedoms and our democracy than teaching our children and youth that "their liberties are the gift of God." Since the academies of Jefferson's day were decidedly religious in both subject matter and orientation, the fundamental truth of man's God-given liberties was an integral part of education below the college level. Jefferson's authorization of religion classes at the University of Virginia, under denominational direction and control, enabled college students to obtain a knowledge of God, of man's relations to God, and an understanding of God's greatest natural gift to man—his freedom.

Our nation cannot preserve its culture, civilization, and freedom if the single most important truth of our heritage may not be transmitted to our children. That which is essential to Western civilization must be an integral part of education. An educational system that is based on the principle of the rejection of Ultimate Truth is false education. It is destructive of both the integrity of the individual person and the fabric of our culture and freedom.

This censorship,[22] this rejection of Ultimate Truth, is the real crisis of our times, intimated Charles Malik, Lebanese Ambassador to the United States. "Without God and without the law of nature, the West cannot save itself, let alone the whole world," he told a Washington University graduation class. "Western civilization, if it is to survive," he emphasized, "must stand for what is genuinely and concretely universal in its heritage. This can only mean in the order of nature the moral law, and in the order of God the Christian message in its concrete plentitude." [23] But "Western civilization" cannot "stand for what is genuinely and concretely universal in its heritage"—"the moral law" and "the Christian message"—when approximately 87 per cent of our school children and youth are forcibly deprived of these integrating truths of our heritag .

When that which has been held sacred and true for centuries is rejected, this is revolution. So it is in Asia today. But not in Asia alone. The essence of this revolution, Malik said, "is to hate the authentic freedom of the spirit, to reject any ultimacy to the individual human person, to subvert the traditional norms of truth and conduct, to split up the total man into sensations and dreams, to reduce reason to conditioned reflexes manipulated in the interests of some arbitrary philosophy enthroned and backed by force, to spurn any objective truth, to deify matter and material security, and to deny the existence of God." [24]

What could better characterize the revolution that has transformed American education than Ambassador Malik's description? It is a mere elaboration of the tenets that charac-

terize secularist education. The philosophy that all too generally pervades modern education is heavily overshadowed with
conformism, it hates "the authentic freedom of the spirit";
it rejects "any ultimacy to the individual human person"; it
subverts "the traditional norms of truth and conduct"; it splits
up "the total man into sensations and dreams"; it reduces
"reason to conditioned reflexes manipulated in the interests
of some arbitrary philosophy enthroned and backed by force";
it spurns "any objective truth"; it deifies "matter and material
security"; and it denies "the existence of God."

Our civilization, our culture, and our freedom can be preserved. But essential means must be used to preserve them.
The brilliant Lebanese ambassador tells us what values must
be inculcated if we are to raise up a generation that can preserve our freedom. "Nothing is more important today than to
know that absolute standards exist and to demonstrate their
existence in theory and life; to instill the sense of individual,
personal responsibility so as to save man from falling into
massive unreason and irresponsibility; and to inculcate the
fear of God so that men might live in the certain presence of
a hidden judge." [25]

Because God and the study of God are of such fundamental
importance to democracy, every democratic state must have
an interest in the religious education of its children and
youth. The basic principles of democracy—such as man's
dignity and worth, man's rights and equality—are fundamentally religious. They have no meaning except as having their
source in God. Consequently, the democratic state which
is interested in its own self-preservation must of necessity be
interested in the religious education of its people. The alternative is inevitable self-destruction, the internal decay of our
commonly accepted values, of our respect for the dignity and
worth of the human person, with a resulting mass totalitarianism in which the individuality of the human person is com-

pletely annihilated. For, as Dr. W. G. Peck has said, "You
cannot have a valid human meaning in a universe which is
meaningless; and you cannot maintain the Christian respect
for persons when you have dismissed the Christian doctrine of
God." [26] Democracy's respect for the human person must be
based in the people's respect for and knowledge of the God
who gave man dignity, worth, and freedom.

Sir Walter Moberly approaches the question another way
when he maintains that "since value-judgments are indispensable to any rational organization of the life of individuals or
of communities, a university training should enhance the
student's capacity to make such judgments intelligently." [27]
The capacity to make intelligent judgments concerning the
most fundamental issues of life presupposes a knowledge of
the nature of man, a knowledge of God, and a knowledge of
man's relations to God to Whom he has obligations and from
Whom he has rights that transcend the scope and power of
civil society. Value-judgments can be made only on the basis
of a point of reference. If this point of reference does not
transcend man's world, then it is this-world centered—it is
*secularized*. And, "Man is the measure of all things."

If "man is the measure of all things," on what basis can we
object to Hitler's extermination of the Jewish minority, or to
the Communist enslavement of eastern Europe, of China, or
of the whole world? If "man is the measure of all things,"
then the most cunning and most powerful man or group of
men will always prevail, and, more than that, they will always
be right. And, peculiarly enough, they will always be right
because they subscribe to the same "tenets" that have characterized secularist education in the United States over the past
fifty years; namely, "*there is no eternal truth; there is no absolute moral law; there is no God.*" This is the philosophy of
power, the totalitarian philosophy that might makes right.

In a free society we cannot accept this slave-state philosophy. The very concept of freedom presupposes that there is

"eternal truth," that there is an "absolute moral law," and that "there is a God." If these presuppositions are not correct, then there is no norm of reference and all values are relative. And if all values are relative, then might makes right, and the individual is just a pawn in the hands of the all-powerful state.

In a free society man's normative judgment must be based on norms that transcend the level of human activity. "If man has the power to define what his standards are," declared Secretary of the Treasury Robert Bernerd Anderson, "then they almost inevitably become what he wills them to be. . . . This, to me," continued Secretary Anderson, "is the great ethical error of materialism, humanism, and all other systems of philosophy which do not recognize the independent existence of absolute moral and spiritual values." [28]

In such a philosophical orientation constitutional guarantees of the rights and liberties of the individual person and statutory provisions implementing them are of themselves of little value. The Stalin Constitution of 1936 contains a declaration of fundamental rights that surpasses in its scope our own Bill of Rights. This is a man-made bill of rights based upon man-made norms and values. Consequently, against the Soviet man-made state, the individual person has no rights. "Written professions of intent cannot be translated into uniformity of meaning unless there is lodged in the public conscience a clear understanding of the deeper values upon which those professions depend for their substance and worth," declared Mr. Anderson. This "clear understanding of the deeper values" upon which legislative enactments are based can be "lodged in the public conscience" only through the long process of education. Such an understanding of abstract principles does not come to the average citizen by way of osmosis.

The "deeper values" upon which man's laws must be based, says Secretary Anderson in harking back to the philosophy of the Founding Fathers, "are spiritual and absolute, rather than material and relative. They are eternal rather than transient. Most important, they are constituted by an Authority quite above and beyond the sphere of human development. If man is to perceive these values as the lasting, immutable works of his God, then the law has a proper foundation. He must not conceive them as the property of his own mind, to be twisted and distorted to suit the demands of expediency." [29]

If we are to preserve our freedom and democracy, these values must form the conscience of America; they must form the conscience of the vast majority of the American people. "The indispensable basis for any law that would secure justice and freedom and equality," points out the Secretary of the Treasury, "is its identity, both in inception and in execution, with the principles of Christian conscience." [30] But such a Christian conscience can be formed only through a long and sincere study of judaeo-Christian teaching. Mr. Anderson gives this injunction: "Study the Sermon on the Mount; the Parables; the Ten Commandments; the Epistles of St. Paul." [31] The values and truths contained in these teachings of Christ must, if they are to form the public conscience, be made an integral part of the education of the individual child and youth. Only such education can preserve for our nation those principles that are essential to the reconciliation of order and freedom.

These principles and values were essential to the conception of freedom; they are essential to its preservation. Secretary Anderson told the students at Baylor University that "the great spread of freedom the world has enjoyed over the past two hundred years and the tremendous material advances which that freedom has engendered, have come about as the result of a general recognition that these great and eternal values are indeed the proper basis for our laws and legal processes." [32]

The Secretary points out that Thomas Jefferson wrote into

the Declaration of Independence this all-important statement: "We hold these truths to be self-evident, that all men
are created equal, that they are endowed by their Creator
with certain unalienable rights, that among these are Life,
Liberty, and the Pursuit of Happiness." This is the philosophy
of our freedom, of our democracy. "We in America," declared
Mr. Anderson, "have asserted our conviction of the Divine
source of a set of absolute spiritual values, and with it we express a conviction that these values must not be subverted by
any man or any government composed of men for any reason
whatever." [33] If our "set of absolute spiritual values" is not to
be lost to our children, we must transmit to our children a
deep conviction of their "Divine source." Without this conviction, without this knowledge, our spiritual values will be
lost and with their loss the very foundations of our freedom
will be undermined.

It appears that most of our educational institutions are
today failing to transmit a knowledge of those fundamental
values that transcend the level of man's activities. As a consequence our college youth, remarked Dr. Henry P. Van Dusen,
are the "products of an age which has absorbed contemporary
information all out of proportion to its equipment to understand it, to interpret it, to appraise it, and to assimilate
it. . . ." [34]

Dr. Van Dusen quotes two students of unusual ability who
analyze modern education with greater penetration and understanding than most of their elders are capable of. (The
students were attending two of our oldest and strongest universities.) One declares:

We of the younger generation grew up in a "practical," "rational"
world. It was so very practical that there was nothing in which it
could believe; it was so very rational that it rationalized its way
into an unruffled view of its own destruction. . . .

It might be expected that in acquiring a liberal education, a
group of young men might find ideas and ideals to which they

could cling with courage and conviction. But such seems not to be the case. Perhaps nowhere is there so much lip service paid to democratic ideals and so little stern devotion to these ideals as in the American colleges. The question forces itself upon us: What are we here for and what is a liberal education striving toward? [35]

The other student, writes Van Dusen, "after reminding the older generation of the framework of *their* upbringing—traditional Christianity and democracy, eternal principles of right and wrong, the existence of the human soul, a personal God and life after death," poses the question:

But what about us, the youth of America? What have we been taught to revere? When *our elders* refer to eternal verities, absolutist ethics, *we* are likely to recall the lesson your instructors in sociology have driven home—that morals are relative to time and place, that what is good in one society is bad in another. . . . Have we not gleaned from your professors of natural science, philosophy and ancient history that religions are the product of myth and superstition and that men create gods in their own image? . . . Biology now conceives of man as one species of mammal. . . . Free will is at odds with the basic assumption of modern science—determinism. . . . Little of the learning we absorb includes value judgments.

Then follow his queries, direct implications of the university's teaching:

If men are but animals, why not treat them as such? If man is a slave to determinism, incapable of free choice, what is the value of the ballot, trial by jury and civil liberties in general? . . . Personally I fail to understand how you can expect us to become ardent Christians and democrats when the vital postulates on which these faiths are supposed to rest are daily undermined in the classroom. . . . Isn't it palpably obvious that the root of the trouble lies in an apparent contradiction between the implications

of our studies and the ideals we are expected to revere? . . . **We,**
the young, are the American tragedy.[36]

It is my conviction that freedom of choice in education
would remedy in part, at least, this American tragedy. It
would enable parents and students to choose schools in which
true "democratic ideals" prevail and in which both faculty
and students have a "stern devotion to these ideals." It would
enable them to choose schools in which "traditional Christianity and democracy, eternal principles of right and wrong,
[and a belief in] the existence of the human soul, [and] a
personal God and life after death" form the framework and
fabric of education. It would enable them to reject schools
that teach that man is but an animal whose every action is
determined by physical laws, and to choose schools that teach
that man is a spiritual being and a son of God, that he has
dignity, value, and worth, that he possesses a free will, that his
freedom of choice makes democracy possible, that he has certain rights that may not be abridged by the state, and that he
has a destiny that transcends the material world in which he
lives.

It is inconsistent with principles of freedom of mind and
freedom of religion to deny educational benefits to children
and students who desire an education that concerns itself
with the whole man, body and soul, and the Whole Truth.
Children and students have a right to study that Truth and to
learn how to live their lives consistent with It. Enforced conformity to educational philosophy that rejects God as a relevant factor runs counter to the principles of democracy and
is inconsistent with personal freedom.

Because of this enforced conformity to a secularized education, "most of the American people are religiously illiter-
ate," [37] says Dr. Bernard Iddings Bell. Writing with a background of more than thirty years of teaching experience on

every level of education, Canon Bell gives the pedagogical reasons for the illiteracy of our people concerning the most fundamental and most lofty truths to which the human mind can aspire. "Our public schools and colleges," he points out, "are rarely antireligious. They simply ignore religion. They look on it as a minor amusement to be practiced by those who find it fun, to be neglected if one desires. Obviously this outlook is quickly communicated to the young. If a child is taught in school about a vast number of things—for 25 hours a week, eight or nine months a year, for 10 to 16 years or more—and if for all this time matters of religion are never seriously treated, the child can only come to view religion as, at best, an innocuous pastime preferred by a few to golf or canasta." [38]

Nevertheless in the minds of many parents and students, religion, as expressed by Van Dusen, is the *"determinative principle in the educational process as a whole,* affecting vitally and decisively the over-all philosophy and content of the curriculum and of its every part, reflecting religion's basic premise that God is the ultimate Ground of Truth in relation to which every segment of knowledge and all particular truths must be oriented." [39] This philosophy gives to religion its proper status in education. It demonstrates the fact that "teaching which does not recognize God as the ultimate Ground of Truth is false teaching." [40]

Knowledge is essentially one piece. It is one by reason of the unity of truth; the nature of each part being determined by the nature of the Whole. But if truth *is* an organic whole, what is the integrating reality? This raises the question of God. Is God the integrating Reality?

Professor Van Dusen gives his profound answer to this question:

To be sure, no human mind, or all together, ever succeeds in encompassing that Whole. But, by the same token, no human mind rightly grasps any fragment of truth without at least some dim awareness of the Whole which gives the fragment its existence and its meaning. Moreover, if Truth be an organism, then every subject and every principal subdivision should be so presented as to suggest that unity. Any segment of knowledge which is portrayed without recognition of its organic relatedness to all other knowledge is being falsely presented. It is not Truth which is being set forth. And, need it be argued, that is unsound education, a betrayal of education's primary and regnant loyalty. As Newman once declared, God has "relations of His own towards the subject-matter of each particular science which the book of knowledge unfolds." [41]

Edward B. Pusey, colleague of Newman, clearly portrayed the implications of this fundamental principle in educational orientation. He wrote:

All things must speak of God, refer to God, or they are atheistic. History, without God, is a chaos without design or end or aim. Political economy, without God, would be a selfish teaching about the acquisition of wealth, making the larger portion of mankind animate machines for its production; Physics, without God, would be a dull inquiry into certain meaningless phenomena; Ethics, without God, would be a varying rule without principle, or substance, or center, or ruling hand; Metaphysics, without God, would make man his own temporary god, to be resolved, after his brief hour here, into the nothingness out of which he proceeded. All sciences . . . will tend to exclude the thought of God if they are not cultivated with reference to Him. History will become an account of man's passions and brute strength, instead of the ordering of God's providence for His creatures' good; Physics will materialize man, and Metaphysics, God.[42]

This comes to the heart of the matter. Formalized courses in religion cannot alone give a knowledge of that integrating Reality which gives unity and coherence to all truth. More than this is needed. "What it demands," writes Van Dusen, "is a fundamental reorientation of *every* subject in the curriculum and its presentation in every course. . . . What is most earnestly urged is that, *if* the basic premise is sound—that Truth is an organic unity and each segment of knowledge what it is by virtue of its place within that unity—then no part of knowledge, whatever its subject matter, will be truly and rightly taught unless that relationship to the Unity of Truth is assumed and, so far as is appropriate, pointed out. And, further, that the educational institution itself which is responsible for the total setting-forth of the *whole* Truth should consciously recognize the basic premise of its undertaking and its responsibility, and acknowledge the Divine Mind without which its enterprise could not take place." [43]

Hastings Rashdall says well that religion or theology *is* the Queen of the Sciences, "the architectonic science whose office it is to receive the results of all other sciences and to combine them in an organic whole." [44] "This is its rightful position," declares the distinguished president of Union Theological Seminary, *"because of the nature of Reality*—because, if there be a God at all, He must be the ultimate and controlling Reality through which all else derives its being; and the truth concerning Him, as man can best apprehend it, must be the keystone of the ever-incomplete arch of human knowledge. Learning which does not confess Him as its Foundation because the Determiner of the conditions which render its enterprise possible, and which does not aspire to Him as its Goal, is false learning, however impressive its achievements and pretentious its claims." [45]

The basic tenets of our "teacher education" are in sharp contradiction to this God-centered theory of education. As indicated above, "some of the most influential tenets" which have characterized secularist education over the past fifty years are: *"there is no eternal truth; there is no absolute moral law; there is no God."* This is the secularization of education; it is the rejection of ultimate Truth, of God-given moral laws, of God Himself.

Under the Constitution any person has the right to adhere to these tenets if he so desires. And as a constitutional right, it deserves the protection of the courts. But I raise the question whether the state has the right to *compel* children to submit to indoctrination in secularist education philosophy, or to any other philosophy, as a condition for sharing in educational benefits. If so, the state can determine what shall be orthodox in philosophy and religion. The Supreme Court of the United States, taking a strong stand in defense of freedom of the mind and freedom of religion in the *Barnette* case, declared, however, that "if there is any fixed star in our constitutional constellation, it is that no official, high or petty, can prescribe what shall be orthodox in politics, nationalism, religion, or other matters of opinion or force citizens to confess by word or act their faith therein." [46]

Sir Walter Moberly, as seen above, spells out the significance of secularized education and its indoctrinating influence on young minds. He writes:

On the fundamental religious issue [the existence of God], the modern university intends to be, and supposes it is, neutral, but it is not. Certainly it neither inculcates nor expressly repudiates belief in God. But it does what is far more deadly than open rejection; it ignores Him. . . . It is in this sense that the university today is atheistic. If in your organization, your curriculum, and your communal customs and ways of life, you leave God out, you teach with tremendous force that, for most people and at most times, He does not count; that religion is at best something extra and optional, a comfort for the few who are minded that way, but among the luxuries rather than the necessities of life. . . . Since it is the habit of the modern university to study all other subjects without any reference to theology at all, the obvious inference is that it does not "admit a God" in any sense that is of practical importance. It is a fallacy to suppose that by omitting a subject you teach nothing about it. On the contrary you teach that it is to be omitted, and that it is therefore a matter of secondary importance. And you teach this not openly and explicitly, which would invite criticism; you simply take it for granted and thereby insinuate it silently, insidiously, and all but irresistibly. . . .

In the assumptions governing curriculum and academic method, the universities today are implicitly, if not intentionally, hostile to the Christian faith and even to a liberal humanism.[47]

If these are the consequences of secularism on the college level, they are also, perhaps even more so, the consequences of secularism on the elementary and secondary levels of education. It is directly in conflict with First Amendment rights of freedom of mind and freedom of religion to compel children to submit to such "all but irresistible" indoctrination as the condition for sharing in educational benefits.

The secularization of elementary and secondary public schools is placed beyond dispute by the decision of the Supreme Court of the United States in the *McCollum* case.[48] The Court there held that the First Amendment prohibits the teaching of religion in public schools. That is, God must be absolutely ejected from the classroom. Will Herberg, noted Jewish writer and educator, declares that "today the *spirit* of public school education is, by and large, *secularist*, even militantly so." [49] And Dr. Bernard Iddings Bell writes, as we have seen, that "as the American school is now conducted, more and more conducted, there is no such thing as religious liberty in American education. There is liberty only to be unreligious." [50] This is liberty only for the secularist.

Dr. F. Ernest Johnson, an official of the Federal Council of Churches, warned that unless religion came to be recognized as a vital factor in the common culture and studied as such in the schools "without imposition or any ecclesiastical sanction," all of American life would become secularized. He declared: "Many Protestant scholars have begun to ask whether the public school will not be maintained at too high a price if the inevitable result is a complacent indifference to religion." [51]

In his address to the Washington Ministerial Union, Professor Johnson of Columbia University spoke of a mobilization which he said all-out secularists seemed to be conducting in the country. He described these people as those "who want the schools not to be merely secular in the sense of indifference to traditional religion and religious instructions, but to adopt an anti-theistic philosophy, a sort of secular religion in which the school becomes in effect a church." [52] That is, the public schools become the state-established church expounding the religion of secularism to captive "parishioners" at public expense.

One of the ironies of the absolute separation of church and state doctrine enunciated by the Supreme Court in the *Everson* case [53] of 1947 is that the doctrine is used to establish a religion in the nation's public schools—the religion of secularism. "I have seen so much recently of this disposition to take over the schools on the part of an aggressive, dogmatic and anti-theistic philosophic movement," observed Professor Johnson, "that I am constrained to call it the most grievous and crudest assault in our time upon the separation of church and state." [54]

Protestant educators and clergymen are becoming more and more concerned about the secularization of American education. Episcopalian Edward McCrady, president of the University of the South, warned that "the education of our future citizens in the Christian way of life cannot be looked upon as anything less than a compelling necessity." [55] But under present educational theory and practice this will not be easy to achieve. "Unfortunately," declared Dr. McCrady, "our tax supported educational system has mistaken freedom of religion for freedom from religion." [56] This view of government education was corroborated by Methodist Bishop Costen J. Harrell, who pointed out that "in recent years we have witnessed an alarming movement toward the secularization of education." [57]

The bishop of Charlotte, North Carolina, declared, further, that "some of the leaders dismiss the idea of God as irrelevant. They replace theology with technology and substitute human smartness for moral and spiritual values. In its extreme form, this approach is blatant paganism. . . ." [58]

The same concern was reflected by Nathaniel F. Forsyth, associate secretary of the Methodist Board of Education. He pointed out that the absolute separation doctrine was being used to deprive children of the right to learn about God. "In our zeal to dissociate church from state we have dissociated religion from the education of the people in public schools." [59]

Religion is necessary for democratic as well as for the personal life of the individual. Moral values cannot be disassociated from religion. This point was made by the Methodist leader the Reverend Thomas J. Van Loon. "Church groups," he said, "have long been bothered by the trend toward secularism which seems discernible to them in public education. . . . Church leaders and public educators alike have been disturbed by the declining ethical standards and sanctions; the lack of a unifying system of values with its resulting fragmentation of culture and personal life." [60]

This decline in "ethical standards and sanctions," this "lack of a unifying system of values," is the inevitable result of education that has removed the only foundation of standards, sanctions, and values—religion. If religion is unimportant, then it follows that all the norms and values that are deeply rooted in religious belief are unimportant. This point was well made by Dr. McCrady when he said: "The almost inevitable impression of a person who has spent 12, 16 or even 20 of the most formative years of his life in the public school system learning there practically everything he knows, without ever hearing religion seriously considered, is simply that it isn't important enough for the government to bother to pay anyone to discuss it." [61]

The president of the University of the South is in complete accord with the English educator Sir Walter Moberly when he takes issue with the "insidious counter-indoctrination which actually pervades most teaching at the college level." He declared:

When the English professor teaches that the moral issues should not be considered in judging a poem or a novel, he is taking a positive stand on a religious subject. When an economics professor teaches that all problems of society are due to monetary factors and can be corrected by economic reform, he is denying the effectiveness of spiritual factors in promoting the Kingdom of God on earth. When a professor of history or politics tells you that statesmen use moral arguments only to conceal their real motives, which are dictated by the selfish struggle for existence, he means to assert the futility and irrelevance or moral considerations; though he inadvertently contradicts himself, since if moral considerations were really without influence in history, they could be of no use as a cover.[62]

Many American parents are convinced that education without God is incomplete, that it deprives the child of the most important spiritual and moral values of life, and that it deprives society of the values that are fundamental for the preservation of our democratic way of life. For this reason an increasing number of parents of every religious faith are making all but heroic sacrifices to send their children to God-centered schools. They are in fact subsidizing the state in order to exercise a constitutional right.

These parents realize that without a knowledge of God the child and the adult alike are adrift, that life has no meaning, and that life's problems are beyond solution. They realize, moreover, that without a knowledge of God there cannot be, in our American society, those fundamental convictions of the brotherhood of man, and of the dignity, worth, and value of the individual person. They realize, furthermore, that unless God is given an important place in the classroom, children will not, with few exceptions, learn their obligations to God and their duties to their fellow men.

To be sure, the primary obligation to teach religion to children rests on the parents. But it certainly is no exaggeration to say that the vast majority of parents fail miserably in the fulfillment of this important duty.[63] In the final analysis, if the child is not taught religion in school, he will receive, with rare exceptions, not much beyond the most elemental religious understanding. Because of this fact, we have become a nation of religious illiterates. "It is undeniable that the young men and women now coming of age in America are for the most part not religious, realize next to no obligation to love and serve God. They are not opposed to religion; they simply do not know enough about religion to have discovered that it has relevancy to life, that it throws light on the meaning of things, that it involves anything much that is of importance to individuals or nations," observed Canon Bell.[64]

Many of these men and women referred to by Canon Bell are the fathers and mothers of today's children. What moral and religious education can they give to their children? If they have no knowledge and love of God, how can they inspire in their children a knowledge and love of God? No one can transmit what he does not possess. Yet, says Canon Bell, these fathers and mothers "would like to give their babies what they themselves have too little gained: some simple and firm hold on a Reality deeper than the flux of that which comes and goes." [65]

It is for this reason, writes the Episcopalian clergyman and educator, that "there are a great many parents, by no means all of them adherents to organized religion, who realize that how to know God has a place, and that no mean place, in a sound education. They perceive easily enough that if human life is to become significant or safe, children as they grow up must somehow learn to dig beneath the superficialities of sensation. They are well aware that a way of living based on nothing more substantial than self-expression and a desire to get on in the world does not lead to poise, sanity, tolerance, inner peace, courage. They understand that, if conduct is not based on search for an Absolute of some kind and on service of that Absolute, morality becomes first a matter of fluid expediency and then a blind obedience to the merely strong." [66]

Yet these parents are not free to give their children a God-centered education. They are pressured by the state to send their children to the public schools where religion may not be taught. The state conditions educational benefits on the surrender of the constitutional right of the parents to send their children to a God-centered school. This is using economic pressures to force parents and children to conform to the theological and philosophical orientation of the state's schools. Religious education can be had only at a price—the price of supporting a second school system.

Children who do not learn their obligations to God and their duties to society will not have much regard for the laws of God, little regard for the laws of society, and none for the rights of their fellow men. Moral principles cannot be divorced from religious principles. When religion is not taught in the American homes and schools, there is no foundation for moral principles. "Neither the Jewish nor the Christian morality is a natural morality," pointed out Canon Bell; "both recognize supernatural demands and rest on supermundane sanctions. . . . If there is no God, to take obvious examples, free love is entirely defensible, and politics based on force is inevitable. Our secularized world denies more and more the validity of a moral code based on anything but expediency. Children soon discover that this is true." [67]

More and more of our Protestant leaders are coming to the conclusion that religious education is necessary for the inculcation of moral and spiritual values. The Church Federation of Greater Chicago declared in a 10,000 word statement that teaching the fundamental principles of religious faith in God "and the consequences of such faith in life" should be an essential part of the educational process in the public schools. "The public schools," the statement said, "have an obligation to recognize in positive and forthright policy and practice the conviction that true moral, ethical and spiritual values are religious values." [68]

This is also, in part, the reason why Dr. Nathan Pusey, president of Harvard University, emphasized in his baccalaureate address of 1958 the importance of religion in education. The most important questions are not the secular ones, he insists, but "the questions which religion answers for her believers by supplying meaning to life, by kindling hope, and by giving through faith in God a basis for ethical behavior." [69]

The public schools must recognize, the Church Federation statement declared, "that God is the ultimate sanction for moral and spiritual values in life," and that the small minority which does not admit God as "the living reality of life" should not be permitted to "veto" such recognition. [70]

Since we have denied most of our children the opportunity to learn about God and His moral laws, it seems both unrealistic and unfair to expect them to live by norms, standards, traditions, and laws that make sense only in the context of a

Judaeo-Christian orientation. We the adults of America are in large measure to blame for juvenile delinquency. We have, among other things, deprived our children of the "religion" and "morality" which our Founding Fathers, and particularly President Washington, maintained were the "indispensable supports" and the "firmest props of the duties of men and citizens." We have created the environment, the culture, to which our children are reacting. They are the products of our society. "Juvenile delinquency is not an indictment of our young people," Unitarian clergyman Walter Donald Kring asserted; "it is an indictment of our culture." Declaring that teenagers are the "products" of a world created by adults, clergyman Kring said that "the problem is that our society is sick within, and this inner sickness shows up vividly in the environment that we produce for our children." [71]

"We must work on the alleviation of social ills with all the direct methods that we can," the Reverend Kring continued, "but more fundamentally we must provide the religious environment in which the individual soul can grow and come close to God." [72] Certainly, the solution, in part, lies in a reorientation of American society to God and God's moral laws. If we teach our children "silently, insidiously and all but irresistibly," as Sir Walter Moberly puts it, that God is of secondary importance, can we the adults of America who have deprived youth of a knowledge of God and His laws justifiably indict delinquents for homicide, rape, auto theft, felonious assault, grand larceny, and so forth?

J. Edgar Hoover attributes the tragic condition of juvenile delinquency "to a lack of religious training." The director of the F.B.I. emphasizes that "there is a necessary connection between crime and the decline of faith and religious practice. When men do not know God and His justice, they do not respect His laws. The way to make people moral is a return to religion." Therefore, reasoned Mr. Hoover, "a sense of moral responsibility founded on religion must be produced in youth to prevent crime and produce a noble citizenry." [73] And the New York City Board of Education declared in its six-point program to combat crime in the schools that in the community's efforts to solve the problem of juvenile delinquency "there is no substitute for the principles of religion and morality." [74]

Human behavior is based on values. The values of Western civilization have their roots deep in the folds of Christianity. They are based on the teachings of Christ. These values cannot endure in our society unless the teachings of Christ endure. And the teachings of Christ cannot endure in our society unless religion is given an important place in the curricula of our schools. The rejection of God and His Moral Law from the classroom is teaching "insidiously and all but irresistibly" that God is of secondary importance. And if this is what we teach in our schools, it is naïve, to say the least, to expect our youth to live according to norms and standards which are, after all, Christian in their rootage and substance.

It should be noted that public school administrators and teachers, since their actions constitute state action, are subject to tremendous pressures and that they are not, consequently, always free to adopt the methods and policies that they themselves feel are necessary for the training and education of youth.

We come now to the fundamental constitutional question. May government deny educational benefits to all children and students who desire to attend schools which operate on the principle of the coherence of all knowledge and the Unity of Truth? In other words, may government impose a condition as a requisite for sharing in educational benefits that demands the surrender of the constitutional right to attend a school that integrates all particular truths with the Whole Truth, God Himself? Or, may government condition its educational benefits on enforced conformity to an educational philosophy that refuses to recognize God as the Ultimate Ground of Truth?

The Supreme Court of the United States has repeatedly declared that government may not condition its benefits and privileges on the surrender of a constitutional right. If this is a valid principle in any area of government activity, it is most emphatically a valid principle in those areas of government activity that touch the human mind and spirit. Government activities in these areas spell the difference between freedom and tyranny. If government may condition participation in benefits on the surrender of freedom of mind and freedom of religion, it is in the position to control the thought and belief of the people. In the final analysis, it makes little difference whether government enforces conformity to a particular philosophy by the conditioned grant of food ration coupons or by the conditioned grant of educational benefits. Both violate freedom of thought, and both ultimately lead to tyranny. "Without freedom of thought," Mr. Justice Frankfurter declared, "there can be no free society." [75]

One of the reasons why it is so difficult to solve the problem of securing freedom of mind and freedom of religion in education is the fact that many people reject the liberties of the First Amendment as they pertain to the parental right to direct and control the education of their children.

There are, moreover, parents who do not want a God-centered education for their children. This is their legal privilege. Not having any absolute convictions themselves, they feel that children should not be exposed to any particular religious belief. Though children may be indoctrinated in the rules of grammar and social conduct, they may not be taught the Ten Commandments and the Eight Beatitudes. This difference of attitude is explained by the fact that while these individuals accept as true the rules of grammar and social conduct, they do not accept as true the teachings of Christ. And since the teachings of Christ are not accepted as true, it would be a gross injustice and tyrannical impertinence systematically to expose the minds of their helpless children to the "prejudices" of their teachers. In a word, there are no religious truths. And since there are no religious truths, to teach religion to children is to pervert their helpless and unsuspecting minds. Hence, they conclude, neither parents nor teachers have the right to teach their children religion. They must let their children grow to adulthood to discover what religion is most socially "acceptable" to them.

Under the Federal Constitution parents have a right so to protect their children from all religious teaching. Any attempt on the part of the state to compel their children to study religion would be a violation of their rights under the First and Fourteenth Amendments.

Very frequently, however, these people's solicitude for freedom from religion extends to their neighbor's children. They want their neighbor's children, as well as their own, to be protected from religion. For this reason they vehemently resist the teaching of religion in state schools even on a released-time basis, and, moreover, they resent and resist to the furthest extent the teaching of religion to children of believers in church-related schools.

These are frequently the people who strongly resist equal educational benefits for children whose parents think that the study of religion is an important and integrating subject. While they demand for themselves the liberty to determine the nonreligious content of their children's education, they are filled with contempt for the liberty of *others*. They may be described as illiberal liberals, or, in a sense, as absolutist liberals. These individuals are aptly described by De Tocqueville when he says that they "do not deny the excellence of freedom, but they wish to keep it all to themselves, and maintain that all other men are utterly unworthy of it." [76] The objection to freedom of choice in education by these individuals rests, in other words, on an absolutist philosophy that aims to control the thoughts and beliefs of their fellow Americans.

It is an elemental conclusion of the First Amendment guarantees of freedom of mind and freedom of religion that the state may not impose a particular religious belief, be it the positive religion of Christianity or the negative religion of secularism, upon even a single individual. Yet this is precisely what is being done in the state's schools. The state is imposing the secularist religion upon all public school children. Moreover, it demands the surrender of freedom of mind and freedom of religion as a condition for sharing in educational benefits. It conditions all its educational benefits on the acceptance of the secularist orientation of truth. In a word, since the secularist religion has been established as the religion of our state schools by judicial decree, the only parents who enjoy freedom of mind and freedom of religion in the choice of school are the secularists and those who prefer a secularist education for their children.

But what of the rights of parents who believe in the Christian or Jewish religion and think that it should be taught to their children in school? May the state run roughshod over their constitutional rights and compel their children to submit to secularist doctrines? The state has no right to impose either the negative religion of secularism or the positive religion of Christianity upon the children and youth of the nation. Furthermore, the state may not force children or students to conform to the philosophical and theological orientation of government schools as a condition for sharing in educational benefits. This is the imposition of an unconstitutional condition for sharing in welfare benefits. It demands that parents and students surrender the constitutional right of freedom of choice in education, of freedom of mind and freedom of religion, as the price of educational benefits. This is a serious violation of the most important and precious rights guaranteed by the Federal Constitution. It subverts freedom and democracy.

Protestant, Catholic, and Jewish parents who object to the philosophical and theological orientation of state-controlled educational institutions have a right to educational benefits that will enable them to send their children to schools that give a God-centered education. And college students who want to orient all particular truths to Ultimate Truth on the basis of their theological and philosophical convictions have a constitutional right to educational benefits that will enable them to attend colleges and universities that recognize God as the ultimate Ground of Truth.

# 6

# Equal Educational Benefits
# for All Through Freedom
# of Choice

*The certificate or tax credit plan ensures the personal right of the individual child or student to share equally in the educational benefits of democratic society.*

If there is one thing that would seem to be beyond need of proof, it is the proposition that all children and students are equal before the law. Each child and student is a citizen of the United States and of the state in which he lives. Each has the right to enjoy the privileges and immunities of his state. But most important of all, each child and student has the right to an equal share in all benefits that his state government provides for the class to which he belongs. The right to share in such benefits is a personal right guaranteed by the Fourteenth Amendment to the Constitution.

A state may have incalculable mineral and oil resources; it may have vast forest reserves; it may be endowed with rich and fertile soil. A state may be wealthy in industrial capacity, in commercial assets, or in business acumen. But its greatest wealth, its greatest assets are its children and youth. The future of America rests with them.

For this and other reasons, the state has an active interest in the religious, mental, moral, and physical development of each one of its children and youth. This explains and justifies the state's interest in education.

The purpose of government in education is to secure the good of the individual child and student and the good of the entire community. With respect to this purpose, all children and students are equal. In its effort to secure this purpose, the state may not classify children and students on the basis of race, religion, or color. Consequently, every child and student has a right to share equally in state educational benefits regardless of his religious belief.

The Fourteenth Amendment to the Constitution guarantees that "no state shall deny to any person the equal protection of the laws." This guarantee, said the Supreme Court, "requires that all persons . . . shall be treated alike, under like circumstances and conditions, both in the privileges conferred and in the liabilities imposed." [1] Legislation meets the demands of the equality clause if it "affects alike all persons similarly situated" [2] with respect to the purpose of the law. With respect to the purpose of education laws—the intellectual good of the individual child and student and the good of the whole community—all students are similarly situated. Hence, in the distribution of educational benefits, the state may not classify children and students on the basis of their exercise of the constitutional right of freedom of choice in education.

It should be obvious but it needs to be emphasized that the right to share equally in educational benefits does not inhere in a school system; it does not inhere in a pile of buildings. The right inheres in the individual child or student regardless of his exercise of freedom of mind or freedom of religion in the choice of school. This is a *personal* constitutional right under the Fourteenth Amendment. "The essence of the constitutional rights," said Mr. Justice Hughes, "is that it is a personal one. . . . It is the individual who is entitled to the equal protection of the laws." [3] That is to say, the right to share equally in educational benefits inheres in the child or student as an individual person, and, since the child or student has a constitutional right to attend an independent school, the right is neither lost nor surrendered when he chooses to attend such a school.

In other words, since the student has equal educational rights and since his choice of school is a constitutional right, the state may not, in the distribution of its educational benefits, classify its children and students into those who attend government schools and those who do not attend such schools. Such classification is an arbitrary discrimination against children and students because of their exercise of a constitutional right. As such it violates the First and the Fourteenth Amendments.

The state, as has been seen, may not demand the surrender of freedom of mind and freedom of religion as a condition for sharing in welfare benefits. The Supreme Court of the United States has set down the principle that the state, in granting privileges, "may not impose conditions which require the relinquishment of constitutional rights." [4] When the state grants educational benefits, it may not impose conditions for sharing equally in such benefits which require the relinquishment of the constitutional right to attend an independent school.

Mr. Justice Jackson emphasized the great importance of the equal protection guarantee as a check on the arbitrary action of government. "I regard it as a salutary doctrine that cities, states and the Federal Government must exercise their powers so as not to discriminate between their inhabitants except upon some reasonable differentiation fairly related to the object of regulation," [5] he wrote. When government is engaged in the distribution of educational benefits, the student's exercise of the constitutional right of freedom of choice in schooling quite obviously does not constitute a "reasonable differentiation" justifying discrimination.

"This equality is not merely abstract justice," continued Justice Jackson. "The framers of the Constitution knew, and we should not forget today, that there is no more effective practical guaranty against arbitrary and unreasonable government than to require that the principles of law which officials would impose upon a minority must be imposed generally. Conversely, nothing opens the door to arbitrary action so effectively as to allow those officials to pick and choose only a few to whom they will apply legislation. . . . Courts can take no better measure to assure that laws will be just than to require that laws be equal in operation." [6]

Consequently, it must be concluded that when government subsidizes the education only of children and students who attend one particular kind of school, its action is "arbitrary," "unreasonable," and discriminatory. The arbitrary classification of students on the basis of their exercise of a constitutional right results in laws that are both unjust and unequal. Students are deprived of their personal constitutional right to share equally in educational benefits because of what they think or believe.

Commenting on this situation, Harvard Law Professor George K. Gardner observed "that a system under which all school children receive the same measure of support from the taxpayers comes closer to reflecting the spirit of the Declaration of Independence and the First Amendment than a system under which the right to receive any measure of support from the taxpayers is conditioned upon attendance at a municipally controlled school." [7]

This arbitrary classification based on what children and their parents think or believe is applied in other areas of welfare legislation as well. Public protection for children against the dangers and hazards of highway traffic, against the inclemency of the weather, and public assistance in traveling long distances in fulfillment of compulsory education laws are denied to children in nearly every state because of what they think or believe. Public health services are denied to children in nearly every state because of what they think or believe. Moreover, state subsidies for hot lunches are denied to children in nearly every state because of what they think or believe. And, finally, tax-provided secular books are denied to children in nearly every state because of their exercise of the constitutional rights of freedom of mind or freedom of religion in the choice of school.

These classifications do not constitute equal protection of the laws; they constitute arbitrary discriminations based on the student's thoughts and belief. This is in violation of the Fourteenth Amendment guarantee of equality. "The guaranty [of equal protection] was aimed at undue favor and individual or class privilege, on the one hand, and at hostile discrimination or the oppression of inequality, on the other hand," [8] declared the Supreme Court.

Classification of students on the basis of their exercise of a constitutional right in the choice of school does not fulfill the constitutional requirement of equal protection. Such a classification is arbitrary because it fails to place in the same category all students similarly situated with respect to the state's purpose in education. It classifies students on the basis of what they think or believe. This is an unreasonable and arbitrary classification. "Arbitrary selection," declared the Supreme Court, "can never be justified by calling it classification. The equal protection demanded by the Fourteenth Amendment forbids this." [9]

It needs to be repeated that the state's purpose in education is the education of individual children and students for their personal good and for the common good. In its efforts to achieve this purpose, the state must use such means as are consistent with constitutional principles and guarantees. It may not adopt means that violate the constitutional rights of individual children and students. Most fundamental among these rights are freedom of mind and freedom of religion. Hence, in fulfilling its educational obligations to all its children and youth, the state must respect the freedom of the individual mind and spirit. If the state undertakes the operation of a government school system, it cannot, consequently, force all children and students to conform to the philosophical and theological orientation of that system. Hence, a governmentally operated school system can never be more than a *partial means* for fulfilling the state's educational obligations in a society that respects freedom of thought and freedom of religion. The state must adopt other means that give proper recognition to the freedom of the human mind and spirit in the pursuit of truth. Such other means must enable the child or student to attend the school of his choice.

It is apparent, therefore, that with respect to the state's purpose in education all children and students are similarly situated. Further, it is apparent that since all classifications in the distribution of welfare benefits must be made with reference to the purpose of the law, a state may not classify its children and students on the basis of race, color, or religious belief. That is to say, if the state wishes to classify its children and students for the distribution of educational benefits, it must discover some ground of difference that makes them differently situated with respect to the state's purpose in education. But since the state's purpose in education is the intellectual development of every individual child and youth, all children and students, no matter what their choice of school, are not only similarly situated with respect to the purpose of the law but identically situated.[10]

Mr. Justice Brandeis stated this doctrine of equality precisely for the Court when he declared that "classification must rest upon a difference which is real . . . so that all actually situated similarly will be treated alike." [11] Furthermore, a classification "must rest upon some ground of difference having a fair and substantial relation to the object of the legislation, so that all persons similarly circumstanced shall be treated alike." [12] If a classification in a law is to meet constitutional requirements, it "must regard real resemblances and real differences between things and persons, and class them in accordance with their pertinence to the purpose in hand." [13] A child's or a student's exercise of his constitutional rights in the choice of school has absolutely no "pertinence" to the state's "purpose" in education. All classifications based on a child's or a student's thoughts or belief, consequently, are arbitrary and unconstitutional. Such classifications deprive the individual child or student of his equal rights under the law.

It may be set down as a fundamental principle that, in the distribution of its benefits, the state must be objectively indifferent to the religious beliefs of its citizens. This principle of freedom was cogently stated by Mr. Justice Alexander in a case involving the power of a state to give textbooks to children attending parochial schools when he said: "In furnishing vaccine for its diseased, shelter for its needy, care for its insane, uniforms for its militia, and protection against 'acts injurious to morals,' the state recognizes needs that are physical, material, moral, and recognizes them with a gaze which throws out of focus any *credal* background." [14]

The constitutional doctrine of legal equality would be meaningless unless it presupposed individual differences. The state, while recognizing its citizens with all their individual differences, must yet treat them all alike. To demand conformity as a condition for sharing in welfare benefits is to negate the whole intent and purpose of the equal-protection clause of the Fourteenth Amendment. Therefore, the state, in the distribution of public funds for the education of its children, must treat all children alike regardless of their thoughts or religious belief. To classify children on the basis of their thoughts or belief is an unconstitutional classification and a violation of the First and Fourteenth Amendments.

The school child and the college student are citizens of their state and as such are entitled to all the privileges of their class. The exercise of freedom of thought or freedom of belief can never be made a test for sharing in such benefits. The application of this fundamental principle was well exemplified by the Mississippi Supreme Court in the *Chance* case where it declared: "There is no requirement that the church should be a liability to those of its citizenship who are at the same time citizens of the state, and entitled to privileges and benefits as such." [15]

If the equal protection of the laws requires that religious belief should not be "a liability to those of its citizenship who are at the same time citizens of the state," it also requires that individual citizens bear the duties and burdens of citizenship irrespective of religious belief. When the Federal Government calls young men to serve in the military during times of war, it does not select them on the basis of religious classification. When the commanding officer sends them into the front lines to die in defense of the liberties of America, he does not select them on the basis of religious classification. And when the government gives the war dead an honorable burial at public expense, it does not deny it to some of the dead because of their religious belief. Yet in the distribution of educational benefits to the sons and daughters of the war dead, government classifies their children on the basis of religious belief. Thousands of fathers have died in defense of the liberties of our nation, but their sons and daughters are denied the basic liberties of freedom of mind and freedom of religion in the choice of school.

When Internal Revenue or tax officials assess a citizen's income, they do so, in Mr. Justice Alexander's phrase, "with a gaze which throws out of focus any *credal* background." They do not exempt a citizen from the income tax because of his religious beliefs. Every man with an assessable income and property is subject to taxation by every level of government, from the Federal Government down to the local school district. Religious belief is no disqualification for the payment of taxes. This is simply to say that in bearing the tax burdens of government citizens are not classified on the basis of religious belief. Yet in the distribution of tax-provided benefits, the sons and daughters of taxpayers are classified on the basis of religious belief. Children and students who exercise their religion in the choice of school are denied all educational benefits.

On the basis of constitutional guarantees, a citizen's membership in a church or his exercise of religion does not relieve the state of its welfare obligations to him. The citizen's rights are not surrendered; the state's obligations remain. "If the pupil may fulfill its duty to the state by attending a parochial school it is difficult to see why the state may not fulfill its duty to the pupil by encouraging it 'by all suitable means,' " wrote Justice Alexander. And the reason for this constitutional injunction, continued the judge, is that "the state is under duty to ignore the child's creed, but not its need. It cannot control what one child may think, but it can and must do all it can to teach the child how to think. The state which allows the pupil to subscribe to any religious creed should not, because of his exercise of this right, proscribe him from benefits common to all." [16]

In the context of the freedom guaranteed by the Bill of Rights, students who exercise their religion in the choice of school should not be proscribed from "benefits common to all." In the distribution of its educational benefits "the state is under duty to ignore the child's creed, but not its need." To refuse to grant this basic principle of freedom of the mind and freedom of religion is to claim for the state the right to control thought and belief. This violates personal integrity; it violates the First and Fourteenth Amendments.

The state, said the Mississippi Supreme Court, "cannot control what one child may think, but it can and must do all it can to teach the child how to think." The certificate or tax credit plan enables the state to "do all it can to teach the child how to think" without demanding the right to control what he shall think. In this context of liberty, the child and student would not be forced to surrender freedom of mind and religion as a condition for sharing equally in the educational benefits provided for a class to which they belong. The certificate or tax credit subsidy to the individual child or student would enable the state to "fulfill its duty to the pupil by encouraging it 'by all suitable means.'"

# 7

# Government Neutrality
# Between Religious and
# Nonreligious Education

*The certificate or tax credit plan enables government to achieve neutrality between religious and nonreligious education.*

The Federal Constitution guarantees freedom of choice in education. This freedom of choice is embedded in the First Amendment guarantee to freedom of mind and freedom of religion. On the basis of these constitutional liberties, parents have a right to send their children to church-related schools and colleges, and children and students have the right to attend such educational institutions.[1]

Yet when parents and children exercise this right, they are deprived of all public educational benefits. Professor Wilber G. Katz put it bluntly when he said that "we exact a price for the exercise of this liberty." [2]

Liberty at a *price*—this is not liberty. This is the suppression of liberty. In human affairs liberty means the freedom to choose alternatives. But religious-minded parents and their children are placed in a dilemma, both horns of which are totally unacceptable. The state-devised dilemma that confronts parents is this: submit your child to a tax-supported secularized education or pay for your child's education elsewhere. There is no freedom of choice in these alternatives. In fact both alternatives involve a violation of constitutional rights. The first alternative violates freedom of mind and freedom of religion. The second alternative, since it deprives children of equal educational rights because of their religious belief, also violates the First Amendment guarantee of freedom of mind and freedom of religion.

"Our public school," argued Mr. Justice Jackson in 1947, "is organized on the premises that secular education can be isolated from all religious teaching so that the school can inculcate all needed temporal knowledge. . . ." [3] This is secularism. That makes secularism the established religion of the public schools. In the *McCollum* [4] decision of the next year the Supreme Court formally ousted from the public schools the positive religions of Protestantism, Catholicism, and Judaism and thus officially established secularism as the religion of the schools. This secularization of public school education Horace Mann strongly opposed in his day. "He took a firm stand against the idea of a purely secular education," writes his biographer Raymond Culver, "and on one occasion said he was in favor of religious instruction 'to the extremest verge to which it can be carried without invading those rights of conscience which are established by the laws of God, and guaranteed to us by the Constitution of the State.' At another time he said that he regarded hostility to religion in the schools as the greatest crime he could commit." [5] The "rights of conscience" to which Mann refers were carefully safeguarded in the Champaign, Illinois, released-time program which came before the United States Supreme Court in the *McCollum* case. But the Court nevertheless ousted all positive religions from the public schools. Horace Mann, let it be repeated, regarded hostility to positive religion in the public schools as the "greatest crime" one could commit.

Religious-minded Protestants, Catholics, and Jews who desire for their children a positive religious education must not only support the established secular religion in government schools, which is a violation of their rights under the First and Fourteenth Amendments, but their children are, moreover, compelled to conform to the established philosophical and theological orientation of the tax-supported schools as a condition for sharing in public educational benefits. This, as has been pointed out above, is a serious violation of freedom of mind and freedom of religion guaranteed by the First and Fourteenth Amendments. Parents who demand for their children an education from which all mention of God has been dehydrated are within their rights under the Constitution. But when government demands that all children conform to this established secular religion of the public schools as a condition for sharing in educational benefits, the children's religious liberty is seriously abridged. This alternative of the dilemma is totally unacceptable to parents of every religious belief who desire a God-centered education for their children.

The second alternative, although it does not involve government dictation as to what children and students shall think and believe, violates freedom of religion since it deprives children and students of equal educational benefits because of their religious belief. This places a burden on the choice of a religious school; it forces parents to pay a second time for their children's education. Such religious tests, burdens, and disqualifications were condemned by Thomas Jefferson in his "A Bill for Establishing Religious Freedom." He declared that "Almighty God hath created the mind free; . . . that all attempts to influence it by temporal punishments, or burthens, or by civil incapacitations, tend only to beget habits of hypocrisy and meanness." [6]

In his great defense of religious freedom Jefferson wrote, moreover, that "no man shall be compelled to . . . suffer on account of his religious opinions or belief; but that all men shall be free to profess . . . their opinion in matters of religion, and that the same shall in no wise diminish, enlarge or affect their civil capacities." [7] But parents who exercise their religion in the choice of school are compelled to suffer on account of their religious opinions or belief. Their children are deprived of all educational benefits; they are forced to pay for the education of their children out of their own pockets. These religious-minded parents can hardly be said to be free in the exercise of their religion. Nor can it be said that their exercises of religion "in no wise diminish . . . or affect their civil capacities," as Jefferson demanded. They are "compelled to . . . suffer" a deprivation of educational benefits for their children "on account of [their] religious . . . belief." Such deprivations are a direct violation of religious liberty; they are in violation of the First Amendment.

The religious-liberty guarantee of the First Amendment is not simply a guarantee against its obliteration. It guarantees the exercise of religion without interference, without obstruction, without the imposition of reprisals or the denial of civil rights because of its practice. The commands of the First and Fourteenth Amendments, declared Chief Justice Stone "extend at least to every form of taxation which, because it is a condition of the exercise of the privilege, is capable of being used to control or suppress it." [8] It makes little constitutional difference whether government controls or suppresses religious exercise by direct taxation or by the indirection of a discriminatory denial of equal rights under the law. If a child or student is deprived of educational benefits because of his exercise of religion in the choice of school, this is a penalty imposed on his religious belief. This penalty compels parents to pay for his education elsewhere. Such "enforced" payments are, like the flat license tax on the distribution of religious literature, "a condition of the exercise of . . . constitutional privileges." And moreover, asserted the Supreme Court, "the power to tax the exercise of a privilege is the power to control or suppress its enjoyment." [9]

Regarding the imposition of burdens on the exercise of religion, the Supreme Court declared that "those who can tax the exercise of . . . religious practice can make its exercise so costly as to deprive it of the resources necessary for its maintenance." [10] Those who can burden the exercise of religion in the choice of school by the denial of educational benefits can make its exercise so costly as to deprive them of the resources necessary to continue to exercise a choice in education. For hundreds of thousands of parents the exercise of religion in the choice of school has been made so costly by the entailed denial of educational benefits to their children that their religious choice in schooling has been completely suppressed. Not only are they deprived of the constitutional right of *freedom* of choice; they have in fact been denied the choice itself.

The power to impose legal discriminations on the exercise of religion is the power to control or suppress its enjoyment. When civil disqualifications and the denial of welfare benefits are directly contingent upon the exercise of religion, government is suppressing the exercise of religion.

When government subsidizes only the children and students who attend state-controlled schools and denies all subsidies to children and students who attend church-related schools, it is throwing the full force of its taxing power in the balance against religious education. Government is not, in fact, neutral between positive religion and the negative religion of secularism. While, on the one hand, its vast financial resources are used to subsidize the education of children in nonreligious schools, the state, on the other hand, denies all educational subsidies to children in religious schools.

Moreover, when government subsidizes education only in nonreligious schools in which secularism is the established religion, it is compelling millions of religious-minded taxpayers to make contributions of money for the propagation of doctrines that are directly in conflict with their own religious beliefs. This, Jefferson condemned. He declared "that to compel a man to furnish contributions of money for the propagation of opinions which he disbelieves, is sinful and tyrannical." [11] Many Protestant, Catholic, and Jewish taxpayers believe, with Henry P. Van Dusen, that "teaching which does not recognize God as the ultimate Ground of Truth is false teaching." [12] They agree, moreover, with Dr. Bernard Iddings Bell that "there is no such thing as religious liberty in American education" and that "there is liberty only to be unreligious." [13] They agree, further, with Dr. Will Herberg that "the *spirit* of public school education . . . is, by and large, *secularist*, even militantly so." [14]

Yet these Protestant, Catholic, and Jewish taxpayers are compelled, contrary to Jefferson's principle of religious liberty, to support the government schools, even though the secularist orientation of the schools is directly in conflict with their most fundamental religious beliefs. They are compelled to support education that engages in "false teaching" because it refuses to "recognize God as the ultimate Ground of Truth," education that deprives all children of "religious liberty" except the secularist-minded, education that is "secularist," that has removed God from the classroom and teaches, as Sir Walter Moberly charges, "silently, insidiously, and all but irresistibly" that God is unimportant.[15] The enforced support of public education by the religious-minded taxpayer falls directly under the condemnation of Jefferson. School taxes "compel a man to furnish contributions of money for the propagation of opinions which he disbelieves."

"It would seem that a believer in religious liberty should support a role of neutrality between religious believers and non-believers," [16] observed Professor Katz. This appears fundamental. Moreover, "everyone agrees that religious freedom precludes the use of penalties and discriminations to induce or reward religious conformity." [17] This appears fundamental also. Yet penalties and discriminations are imposed on the religious nonconformist in the choice of school, while orthodoxy and conformity are rewarded. Such enforced conformity is in conflict with the constitutional requirement of government neutrality between religious believers and non-believers. The United States Supreme Court declared, as a matter of fact, that the "First Amendment requires the state to be neutral in its relations with groups of religious believers and non-believers; it does not require the state to be their adversary. State power is no more to be used so as to handicap religions than it is to favor them." [18]

The all but total failure of the several states to meet these standards of neutrality is one of the greatest anomalies in the enforcement of our Bill of Rights. It is one thing to enunciate principles of liberty in a Bill of Rights; it is another thing to enforce those principles in the political arena. This is only to say that principles of law are not always the ultimate determinants of what is done politically.

The Federal Government has, on the whole, achieved a far greater degree of neutrality between religion and nonreligion than have the states. This is particularly true of Federal legislation in the field of education. In providing for the education of veterans, Professor Katz points out, "Congress left veterans free as to their choice of school and profession. . . . And not even the most enthusiastic 'separationist' criticized this policy or questioned its constitutionality." [19] This neutrality on the part of the government enabled the veteran to attend the school of his choice, whether denominational or nondenominational, at the government's expense.

The G.I. Bill of Rights gave the individual veteran freedom of choice in education, but it gave him more than this. It gave him freedom in the choice of professional training. "The result of the 'GI bill' was thus to place vocation to the ministry financially on a par with vocation to medicine or the law," [20] writes Professor Katz. This is the par excellence example of neutrality; it is also the par excellence example of freedom of choice in education. On the state level, however, we fall far short of neutrality and freedom of choice. In the words of Professor Katz: "Provision of heavily subsidized courses in law and medicine in state universities weights the scales against religious vocations. . . ." [21]

It is axiomatic that the Founding Fathers adopted the First Amendment prohibiting the establishing of a national church to make it easier to achieve the free exercise of religion for all citizens. That is, the religious liberty of the individual was paramount; "no establishment" of religion was secondary and instrumental to this. Yet today the *Everson* reinterpretation of the "no establishment" clause into an *absolute* separation doctrine is actually used to deprive the individual citizen of his *religious liberty*. This point is well made by Law Professor Katz in the following passage of his article on "The Freedom to Believe:"

We come finally to questions as to elementary schools conducted under religious auspices. Let me say immediately that I think we have here applied the separation principle in a way which hampers the exercise of religious freedom. In 1925 the Supreme Court held unanimously that the constitutional liberty of parents includes a right to send their children to religious schools. But we exact a price for the exercise of this liberty. This is the result of our policy of taxing for the support of public education alone, and of our failure to provide tax deductions or offsets for any part of tuition paid to religious schools.[22]

The Supreme Court has repeatedly declared that the First Amendment freedoms occupy a preferred position; that is, these liberties are so valuable that any state law restraining or suppressing them must be carefully scrutinized by the courts. And Jefferson maintained that among these liberties, religious liberty was most lofty. Nonetheless, it is religious liberty that is sacrificed on the altar of the new *Everson* doctrine of *absolute* separation of church and state. This is a reactionary absolutist doctrine that enables the state to suppress and restrain religious liberty in the field of education. Professor Katz agrees with this analysis when he asserts that we should "stop claiming that absolute separation is a libertarian ideal, and to admit what is lost when we abandon government neutrality towards religion and freeze in constitutional form a separation of church and state which restrains the free exercise of religion." [23] Thus is the most fundamental of our liberties eroded and suppressed.

The International Union for Freedom of Education adopted a resolution in 1953 calling for freedom of choice in education. It declared that governments have a strict duty in justice to aid all parents financially in educating their children in the schools of their choice. The International Union based its conclusion on the fact that the right of parents to complete freedom of choice in the education of their children is not an empty liberty, but one that involves the corresponding duty to achieve the right. The corresponding duty to make it possible to achieve this right rests on government. The resolution of the Union is based on neutrality between religion and nonreligion. It did not in one resolution proclaim the principle of freedom of choice in education, and in the next proclaim principles designed to penalize parents for their exercise of this freedom.[24]

Such lofty principles of religious liberty as the International Union adopted are rejected by the several governments of America. The states have rejected the position of neutrality between religion and nonreligion; they have thrown the weight of their taxing power behind nonreligious education. This places parents who believe in religious education in a most disadvantageous position. Moreover, this discriminatory action enables the state to achieve a suppression of religious education to a degree that it could not, under the Constitution, achieve by direct attack. Professor Procter Thomson, referring to this important issue, writes: "But private schools in general and church-related schools in particular are, so to speak, taxed by the conditions of choice facing the individual who contemplates sending his children to one of them, that is, the double burden he must thereby assume. . . . This subtle discouragement to religious-based education is a way of accomplishing indirectly what could or would never be done overtly and by announced intent." [25]

Dr. Bell is emphatic in his espousal of state neutrality between religion and nonreligion. He objects to the state's lack of neutrality in subsidizing education that satisfies the demands of nonbelievers alone. He declares that if our public schools have to be officially nonreligious, "then the only decent thing is to permit religious groups to run their own schools, which of course we now do, and to give them tax money to run them with, which we do not." [26]

The constitutional principles of religious liberty compel to this conclusion. They can lead to none other. The conclusions cannot be avoided. Virtually no democracy in the West, save the United States of America, has so adamantly stood face to face with its principles of liberty and refused to recognize in them the simple conclusions of educational freedom. America virtually alone of all the West demands the surrender of religious liberty as the condition for sharing in educational benefits. "There isn't a modern democratic society in Europe," Dr. Reinhold Niebuhr declared, "that doesn't give children [in independent schools] more tax support than we do." [27]

Most citizens are so accustomed to state lack of neutrality in the distribution of its educational benefits, and their thought on the matter has been so effectively propagandized, that they think that American educational policy is consistent with principles of liberty. This is regrettable, and it can only be hoped that we Americans will soon discover how far short we fall in practice from achieving the liberty and freedom we so valiantly profess. There are, however, many Americans who follow these principles of freedom to their logical conclusions with a consistency that does not falter because of different religious convictions. Their principles of liberty have a universality that demonstrates a sincere and true dedication to the Bill of Rights. The integrity of these men is in sharp contrast to the conduct of those so-called liberals who profess their dedication to the defense of liberty—all liberty, that is, except the religious liberty of the minority they despise. Here prejudice, not principle, is the guide.

Will Herberg writes of men who believe in religious liberty as it applies to freedom of choice in education but who do not, in the present American context, have the fortitude to express their convictions publicly. Many leading non-Catholics have repeatedly conceded that the religious liberty of parochial school children is being violated. Dr. Herberg, speaking of the Catholic claim for equal educational benefits for their children, observes in *Commentary* that "this attitude is more or less in line with the practice prevailing today in Canada, Great Britain, and other countries, where denominational schools regularly receive support from the public funds." Dr. Herberg then makes the following interesting observation: "And it has been advocated in this country by many non-Catholics, by some even who are devoid of any religious concern but are moved by considerations of what they take to be equity and the public welfare. I recall a surprisingly large number of people with whom I discussed the matter, people of all shades of opinion, who, 'off the record' and 'in principle,' substantially endorsed the Catholic claim. . . ."[28]

In the interest of freedom and justice these men may some day, it is hoped, have the hardihood to defend the rights of their fellow Americans, regardless of their religious beliefs, "on the record" and in the market place. This is the necessary condition for the preservation of freedom. When the majority of citizens tolerate a public educational policy that conditions educational benefits on the surrender of freedom of thought and freedom of religion, liberty is in the process of decay. Liberty cannot long withstand enforced conformity that destroys freedom of mind and freedom of spirit. Enforced conformity is the hallmark of totalitarianism; democracy cannot long endure its crushing embrace, for it destroys individuality and makes of many individuals one homogeneous mass. This marks the end of individual freedom; it marks the end of a free society.

# 8

# Direct Educational
# Subsidies and Society's
# Obligations in Education

*The certificate or tax credit plan enables society itself to pay for the benefits which it receives from the education of children and young men and women, in private and church-related schools and colleges.*

Society has an interest in education because the education of children and young men and women confers advantages upon society as a whole. This fact is the legal justification for the spending of public funds for education—the education of the young serves a public purpose. It is for these community advantages or benefits that society pays when it provides education for the individual. In other words, the individual who is educated at public expense is not the sole recipient of the benefits of his education. The education of the individual member of society redounds to the advantages of society itself.

The benefits that accrue to society from the education of its members are spiritual, moral, political, material, and cultural. These benefits are obviously not departmentalized segments of knowledge; they are the areas, by no means mutually exclusive, of the impact of education upon the life of the community.

Since moral principles cannot be considered apart from the spiritual, the two may properly be considered together. "Neither the Jewish nor the Christian morality is a natural morality; both recognize supernatural demands and rest on supermundane sanctions," pointed out Canon Bell.[1]

A knowledge of God, an understanding of man's relations to God, an intellectual grasp of the moral principles that flow from this relationship, and the reasoned acceptance of these principles are, for the average person, the fruit of prolonged study. And prolonged study means for the normal American child and youth, with few exceptions, the inducements and circumstances of organized education. For this reason the Founding Fathers provided schools even in the wilds of the sparsely settled territories—that the children of the frontiersmen might receive training in "religion, morality, and knowledge."

Our democratic society presupposes, in its day-to-day functioning, basic principles of morality. These principles underlie our philosophy of the dignity and worth, the integrity of the individual person; they give substance and meaning to the basic distinction between right and wrong, between truth and falsehood, between justice and injustice. Without these principles, the orderly conduct of human intercourse, whether on the business, occupational, social, professional, or political level, would be impossible.

These moral concepts are essential to democracy. To the extent that the student gains an intellectual understanding of these moral values during the years of his education, society is directly benefited by the education of the child and student. The foundations of democratic society are secured. The greater the intellectual grasp of these principles, the more surely will our liberties and our democracy be preserved.

If the fundamental principles of our democracy which are

set forth in the Declaration of Independence—namely, "that all men are created equal, that they are endowed by their Creator with certain unalienable rights . . . that governments are instituted to secure these rights"—will be preserved in the hearts and minds of the American people, it will be largely because our educational institutions have given our children and youth an understanding of God, of man's relations to his Creator, of man's God-given rights and duties, and of his consequent dignity and importance as a person and citizen.

In the global struggle between tyranny and freedom, religion and religious education are of fundamental importance. This struggle is, as President Eisenhower pointed out in his commencement address at Mount St. Mary's College, a "struggle between atheistic communism and every kind of free government which has its true roots in a deeply felt religious faith." [2] Hence, those American institutions which help to transmit a belief in God and the moral consequences of such belief are rendering an incalculable service to democracy and Western freedom. "Since," declared the President, "if we believe in human dignity, the value of the individual's soul, if we believe in every right which our founders said was given to us by our Creator, then we must hold fast to the conviction that this struggle of ours is truly a combat between this religious faith and an atheistic doctrine." [3]

If man's God-given gift of freedom is to be successfully defended, its source and nature must be understood. This supposes a knowledge of God and man's relations to God. For this reason, President Eisenhower could say with deep conviction that "I personally think that the traditions of the religiously oriented college become more and more important. As I pointed out, I believe that the core of the struggle between the free and the despotic world today is that between a religious faith and an atheistic dictatorship. If this is true, then I can see no limits to the possibilities of this type of college, where faith in our God is put at the very cornerstone of all that we hope to achieve—all America, or any one of us individually." [4]

In addressing the graduates of the United States Naval Academy, President Eisenhower re-emphasized the importance of moral and spiritual understandings for the national welfare. "I would emphasize the need for developing yourselves as effective leaders in the moral and spiritual realm of life," he told the Annapolis graduates. "It will help you to live up to the finest traditions of the service and of the nation to which you have dedicated your life." [5]

We cannot hope to preserve our freedom in the conflict with totalitarianism unless we know the foundations of personal and national freedom. "Because of the threat imposed by a militant and aggressive atheism, I believe that the strengthening of all phases of our moral and spiritual foundations has a profound significance for the security of our nation," declared the President. "Basic to our democratic civilization are the principles and convictions that have bound us together as a nation," he continued. "Among these are personal liberty, human rights, and the dignity of man. All these have their roots in a deeply held religious faith. They are the convictions that meant more to our founding fathers than did life itself. These are the truths with which we must combat the falsity of Communist materialistic doctrine. Free world respect for them and Communist disdain for them are the very core of the struggle between Communist imperialism and Western freedom. The stronger we become spiritually, the safer our civilization." [6]

On the basis of this criterion, those educational institutions which teach children and young men and women the profound truths of religion and the unchangeable principles of morality are making an essential contribution to the security

)f our nation and the preservation of Western civilization.

Democracy, moreover, presupposes a citizenship that is ;ufficiently well educated to enter into the political life of the 1ation at least on the elemental level. The citizens should be ntelligent enough to vote with discretion, to understand, at east in broad outlines, the important political issues, and to )articipate, in a small measure, in the formation of public )pinion. In view of the citizen's role in our democracy, the )etter educated are the citizens, the better should be the func-:ioning of our democratic society.

The education of the individual redounds to the benefit of the political life of the community. If we are to have govern-ment by the people, we must have a citizenry that can perform the essential functions of a self-governing people. This de-mands an understanding of the issues. But citizens as a gen-eral rule cannot grasp the meaning and significance of the vital issues of the day unless they have associated, during the years of their education, with the great minds of the past and present. Moreover, students must, under the direction and guidance of their teachers, ponder the conflicting views of men, exchange and weigh ideas, search and push forward the frontiers of knowledge, think and, through long and careful reflection, apply the basic principles of life to the problems that constantly confront man. This is education; this is edu-cation's contribution to the political life of society.

Well educated industrial leaders, businessmen, professional and occupational men and women are to a large degree re-sponsible for the material, intellectual, and physical well-being of the community. The education and training of these leaders, even during their formative years, confers benefits beyond measure upon the whole society.

Highly trained mid-twentieth century business and occupa-tional men and women have received a formal education. The schools that participate in the formation of such men and women perform a public function. It is not an unwarranted claim to say that these educated individuals are the backbone of the community. In their professional excellence, all share to a greater or lesser degree. Their activities in democratic society redound to the welfare of the entire social composit in a thousand different ways. The schools that educate these men and women render to a community a public service of incalculable value. They serve a public purpose.

It goes without saying that the cultural level of any society is determined in large measure by education. Consequently, it may be said that the culture that characterizes any community is largely, though not exclusively, an outgrowth of education. The cultural values that impregnate society are an indication of society's indebtedness to the educational institutions that have educated its members.

Society's most important assets and characteristics are the result, directly or indirectly, of the education of its citizens. And the education of citizens is, in the final analysis, chiefly due to the educational institutions that serve the community. In other words, the community is indebted to educational institutions, directly or indirectly, for all those assets and endowments that distinguish a civilized society from a primitive tribe.

Now quite obviously these benefits do not come to the community from state education alone. They come to society no less from private and church-related education than from state education.

In discussing the role of the church-related elementary and secondary school, the Jewish scholar Will Herberg writes:

Parochial schools are, in fact, public institutions, though they are not governmentally sponsored and operated. They perform a public function, supplying large numbers of children with an education that is everywhere taken as the equivalent of the education given in the public schools. They have full public recognition as educational agencies; their credits, diplomas and certificates have exactly the same validity as those issued by governmental establishments.[7]

If church-related schools perform a public function, rendering a service to the whole community, do they not have a claim to a share of public educational funds? Mr. Herberg answers the question:

Since [church-related schools] are thus publicly recognized educational institutions, performing a public educational service, why should they not receive public support? Catholic parents, and many Protestant and Jewish parents as well, who send their children to religious schools of their own choosing, cannot but feel the injustice inflicted upon them when public assistance is refused to the institutions they build for the performance of an acknowledged public service.

Justice, I think, is entirely on the side of those who call for public support to parochial and other religious schools performing a public function; so also is the practice of other democratic countries, where, almost without exception, religious schools meeting the set requirements are given public support as public institutions.[8]

Nonetheless, under our present system of subsidizing education, organized society pays only for the benefits that it receives from the education of individuals in government educational institutions. It does not pay for the benefits that it receives from the education of children, of young men and women, in independent institutions of learning. This it fails to do. Society is receiving incalculable benefits from independent education for which it refuses to pay.

There are, however, people who maintain that society derives no benefits from the education of children, of young men and women, in independent schools and colleges. And it is argued that since education in independent schools and colleges is not beneficial to society, it serves no public purpose. And if it serves no public purpose, society should not and cannot pay for it.

It is of course a privilege to be denied to no one to assert that the education of Washington, Jefferson, Madison, Hamilton, and other leading statesmen, since it was received in church-related colleges, was totally and entirely unbeneficial to American society. The education of these men and their compatriots was heavily interlaced with theology, ethics, and natural-law philosophy; [9] but, if we study the Declaration of Independence, the Federal Constitution, and the early development of our nation, the question may at least be raised whether America suffered irremedial harm on this account. It is true that these men had an unusual sense of the dignity and worth, the integrity and transcendent value, of the human person, and that they believed that God had endowed man with certain inalienable rights, and that, consequently, the powers of government were limited, but freedom and democracy do not seem to have wilted on the vine because of these infectious natural-law viruses.

The signers of the Declaration, products all of church-related schools and colleges, were praised even by their contemporaries not only for the performance of great deeds but also for the virtues and principles that underscored their lives and impregnated their actions. Robert Walsh, a prominent literary man and editor of a series of magazines, wrote in his book *Didactics* in 1836:

If the Declaration of Independence be, of itself, excellent and glorious, it is rendered more so by the characters of the signers; not such as they are lauded by chosen encomiasts, but as they are proved to have been by their performances, their sacrifices, and those remains, originally of a private nature but now divulged, which lay bare their secret feelings, thoughts and designs, unsusceptible of doubt or misconstruction. The degree in which they acted, so perilously and strenuously, upon *principle*, not less than sentiment, and with reference to probably future, rather than present or personal ills, is unparalleled in the examples of collective public virtue. They pledged their lives and property, made prodigious efforts, underwent the sharpest trials, *voluntarily and mainly for abstract right; for the mere sense of regulated liberty, and for the political dignity, more than the vulgar welfare, of their descendants. All their political speculation, too, had a sure anchorage in religion, morals, law and order.*[10]

These men were educated in an old-fashioned curriculum. This curriculum was solidly based on the principles and truths of Christianity as they applied to both personal and civic life. It was the Scholastic method, developed in the medieval universities, which "taught principles rather than facts," "drilled in thinking rather than in memorization." [11] This method of education was not unproductive of men whose lives and works did more to conceive, bring forth, shape and form our nation than any other generation of American citizens. The Harvard Board of Overseers said of their university in 1780: "Many persons of great eminence have by the blessing of God been initiated in those arts and sciences which qualify them for public employment both in Church and State." [12] In educating men for God and country, did not Harvard serve the welfare of the community?

There are today statesmen and leaders in government, business, labor, and the professions too numerous to mention who were educated in private and church-related schools. Many of them were educated from primary school through college, professional and graduate schools in independent institutions. Their learning, virtue, skill, initiative, and dedication to the principles of American democracy make these men great assets to their community and to American society. Their education, which in part made them the men they are, redounds to the benefit of society.

Millions of young men, products of private and church-

related schools, have taken up arms in defense of their coun
try. Society has no greater asset than the man who shields i
against attack with the life of his own body. In the defense
of our country, none surpassed in valor the man who wa
educated to love both God and country. To say that the
education of these millions of men was not and is not a benefi
to society is surely not to speak with the wisdom of a Solomon

Society has an obligation in justice and fairness and unde
the Federal Constitution to pay, or at least to offer to pay
for the benefits which it derives from the education of chil
dren, of young men and women, in private and church-relate
schools. To force parents of children and students attending
independent educational institutions to pay for these com
munity benefits is unfair, unjust, and discriminatory. It i
particularly unfair, unjust, and discriminatory since this com
pulsive payment is directly consequent upon the exercise of a
constitutional right guaranteed by the First and Fourteenth
Amendments.

"Society as a whole," Marion B. Folsom, Secretary of
Health, Education, and Welfare, said, "benefits from the edu
cation of each individual, and it is only proper that society
share . . . the cost of his education." [13]

The certificate or tax credit plan enables society to pay, at
least in part, for the benefits which independent education
confers upon it by enabling children and college students to
pay tuition charges that approximate the cost of education in
the school of their choice.

# 9

# Competition in Education
# Through Freedom
# of Choice

*The certificate or tax credit plan would, through the intro-
duction of competition in education, bring about an improvement of the quality of education throughout the nation.*

The launching of the Soviet satellites and the subsequent
publication of information on the Soviet educational system
have jolted the American people into the realization that
what the mid-twentieth century demands more than anything
else is *quality*. If we are to survive, educators must leave the
mediocrity of "life adjustment" behind and undertake the
intellectual development of our children and youth to their
highest potential.

The efforts necessary to achieve this difficult and long-term
task cannot be induced by fear of communism alone. Fear is
not an enduring and pervasive incentive to inspire unrelent-
ing effort on the part of millions of individuals. Fear is not
an adequate motive for the continued performance of difficult
tasks on the plane of excellence. The slave driven by the fear
of his master did not perform at a high level. Neither will our
American educational system perform at an appreciably
higher level by reason of a new fear of communism induced
by recent Soviet achievements in the scientific world.

We must appeal to something that is typically American to achieve the difficult task of lifting ourselves up by our intellectual bootstraps. *We must appeal to the competitive spirit of free enterprise.* We must bring to the education of the young the challenge of competition. It is this challenge that has created in America a productive and sales efficiency unsurpassed throughout the world. The challenge of competition has instilled into our economy the initiative, the ingenuity, the imagination, the dedication, and the enterprise that have resulted in unequaled excellence.

There can be no complacency with things as they are in a free enterprise system. There can be no contentment with mediocrity. There can be no satisfaction with an inferior-quality product. There can be no acceptance of below-standard workmanship on the production line. While in a socialized economy, all these deficiencies can and do exist, in a competitive economy such a state of affairs would quickly bring about business failure and bankruptcy.

In our free enterprise system every producer of automobiles, every producer of television sets, every producer of refrigerators, must meet the challenge of his competitors' products and ultimately his competitors' ingenuity, inventiveness, imagination, and initiative. In meeting this challenge each producer markets commodities which challenge his competitors in the open market place. There the buyer's freedom of choice is the ultimate test of the quality of his product.

In a nation that is dedicated to free enterprise, education below the college level has, nonetheless, been almost completely socialized. It is almost completely state-owned, operated, and controlled. This eliminates the challenge of competition from an area in which challenge is of vital importance. This removes from our educational system the challenge of equaling and surpassing the quality and excellence of competitors' products. Government monopoly in education, as in business, destroys that initiative, ingenuity, imagination, and enterprise that, in the American competitive system, have enabled business to produce and market goods of unsurpassed quality in the open world market even while paying wages considerably higher than those of most competitors.

Neither industrialists nor government officials think that monopoly—state or otherwise—is capable of producing the best commodities. We think that competition is essential. If we are to produce at our highest potential in the field of education, competition is essential there also. In education, as in other fields of human endeavor, human nature seems to do best when it must meet the challenge of competition. All the breast-beating about the low quality of American education since the launching of the Soviet satellites has been concerned with the low quality of performance on the elementary and secondary levels of education. It is significant that little criticism has been directed at our colleges and universities. The low quality of performance is found precisely on those levels of education in which there is found virtually no competition.

Under such conditions, when government monopoly schools, with educationists in control, adopt a "life adjustment" program offering from eighty to ninety subjects, parents can look to no competitive schools that emphasize such basic subjects as grammar, mathematics, physics, foreign and classical languages, history, chemistry, and literature. While the few independent schools that offer a basic curriculum turn away from two to four applicants for every one they accept, a system of education that is not forced to justify its program in a competitive market place has drifted further and further away from giving our youngsters the basic education that would enable them to enter college and undertake a solid and difficult course of studies. Thus handicapped, too many of our college students are ill-equipped to engage in the difficult scientific and liberal arts programs of our institutions of higher learning. As a consequence our nation is today suffering from a lack of top-notch scientists, creative engineers, and intellectual leaders with a grasp of history and an understanding of the language and culture of other peoples around the world.

If government subsidized the child and student, competition would be introduced into American education. The certificate or tax credit plan would subsidize the demand; that is, it would subsidize the individual child and student. With government subsidy in hand, the individual child and student, enjoying freedom of choice in education, would go to the market place of education. Enabled to purchase his education at any qualified school, he would, in a buyer's market, force the suppliers of education to compete in excellence for his patronage. If parents thought that they could get the best education possible for their children at government schools, they could exercise freedom of choice by sending their children to these schools. But if they thought that the independent schools of their community offered a better program for their children, they could exercise their constitutional right of freedom of choice and register their children in such educational institutions.

Such competition between government and independent schools would be a healthy rivalry that would do much to elevate the educational quality of both. Under our present policy of subsidizing only the children who attend state educational institutions, government schools have no competition since most children have no money to pay tuition at independent schools. Consequently, the number and quality of private and church-related schools are such as to offer for the most part no real competition to the government's schools.

Competition is part of the American credo. It is a corollary of our free enterprise system. Yet in that activity in which competition is essential if we are to achieve our highest excellence, we have little free enterprise and virtually no competition. If there existed in the educational market place different educational institutions in which parents might enter their children and pay their tuition in part with a government certificate or tax credit, we would have a situation in which the different schools would compete with one another in giving the best education possible. Parents could shop around for the kind and quality of education that would best develop the talents of their children. They would not be forced, by economic pressure, to enter their children in schools that are part of a socialized educational system in which the all-important stimulus of challenge is virtually unknown.

Under a competitive system of education, a school would prosper or not on the sole basis of educational performance. If a particular school did not give the mathematical, scientific, religious, social, or liberal education that parents demand for their children, it would soon find that its competitors were outbidding it in the educational market place.

On the other hand, if a particular school or system specialized in giving a "life adjustment" program of education, it would be satisfying the demands of those parents who are convinced that such an education is best for their children. Such an education, however, could not be imposed upon all children in disregard of the rights and wishes of parents, the needs of American society, and the demands of education-for-survival. Furthermore, freedom of choice in education would restore to parents a considerable portion of the right to direct and control the education of their children.

Speaking of education, Professor Friedman observes that "here, as in other fields, competitive private enterprise is likely to be far more efficient in meeting consumer demands than either nationalized enterprises or enterprises run to serve other purposes." [1]

Under the certificate plan, reasoned Professor Thomson, "people would specialize in the kind of education which conformed to their separate preferences. The school system which offered extensive instruction in the United Nations would attract its appropriate quota of clients; those which emphasized Bible-reading, or the core curriculum, progressive education, or traditional academic training would be appropriately favored or disfavored by the judgment of the market." [2]

The certificate or tax credit plan would help to eradicate the totally undemocratic evil of coerced conformity that now characterizes education in America. "The interjection of competition would do much to promote a healthy variety of schools," writes Professor Friedman. "It would do much, also, to introduce flexibility into school systems." [3]

Such competition in the educational field would, as in the industrial economy, give us not only schools of the highest quality, but it would actually bring about the improvement of all schools. Parental freedom of choice would establish a buyer's market in the market place of education; every type of school would be forced to offer the best education possible. This is the effect of competition.

While Dr. Arthur Bestor, historian and educator, found the quality of public school education low in the Middle West and on the Pacific Coast, it is his impression that "the public-school system is best on the eastern seaboard today—in New England, New York, New Jersey and Pennsylvania." Professor Bestor attributes this partly "to the competition of the great private schools of the region, which maintain, on the whole, the consistently highest standards to be found in secondary education in America. Graduates of these schools are in direct competition with those from public schools, and this has an important effect in upholding the quality of all the schools in the region." [4]

The certificate plan would, furthermore, curtail government

interventions in the processes of thought development; the child, under the direction of his parents, would be *free* from governmental pressures in the pursuit of knowledge. This is the position taken by the nineteenth century liberal John Stuart Mill. Whatever else might be said of Mill, he was consistent in his liberal philosophy when he approached the question of the state's function in education. His whole philosophy of liberty rebelled as we have seen against state monopoly in those activities that touch the human mind and spirit. And according to his view, diversity of education was seen to be imperatively necessary for achieving that diversity in opinions that is essential for democracy. For this reason Mill condemned a socialized system of education in no uncertain terms. And he admitted the state into the educational function only to serve as a yardstick of private education.

It has been said with a great deal of truth that the core of our nation's economic progress has been in free enterprise competition. It is also undoubtedly true that the deficiencies of American elementary and secondary education are due to a considerable degree to monopoly conditions and that education could be immeasurably improved by the introduction of free enterprise competition.

The challenge of competition is what is needed in education in America. The complacency of monopoly is the antithesis of the initiative and enterprise essential for the production of a quality product. This complacency is particularly characteristic of a government monopoly created by discriminatory laws against free enterprise. Since government conditions the receiving of educational benefits on attendance at its own schools, it is using an unfair economic coercive pressure to cripple free enterprise in education. As a consequence, free enterprise in education is being forced, as the price of existence, to subsidize the buyer in the educational market place.

The tax credit or certificate plan would give the child or

student freedom of choice in education. He could select his school on the basis of excellence demonstrated by the quality of its products. He would not be forced to attend a monopoly school system that does not have to meet the challenge of competition to force it to perform at its highest potential.

As General Motors would be the last to advocate monopoly in the auto industry as the best guarantee of quality in the production of cars, so also, it may be hoped, a large number of public school teachers and administrators would be the first to advocate free enterprise in education, based on freedom of choice, as the best guarantee of quality in the education of our children and our young men and women.

# IO

# Freedom of Choice in Education Is Fundamental to Liberty

*The certificate or tax credit plan, while making possible freedom of choice in education, would help to preserve our other highly cherished liberties.*

"When it is no longer possible for a man to find a school for his boy except within a universal school system," declared Harold W. Dodds when president of Princeton University, "it will be too late to worry about freedom as we have known it, for it will be gone." [1] Our freedom as a nation is directly consequent upon a real existing choice in education. If ever government uses its legal force effectively to compel conformity in thought and belief, we shall have lost our freedom. We shall then be shaped and molded according to the dictates of a majority will that has jettisoned the Bill of Rights.

Though a choice in education continues to exist, it is, for the average American, a luxury that most cannot afford. It is a luxury that most cannot afford because the exercise of choice in education is not free; the choice entails the penalty of deprivation of public educational benefits. This imposed penalty on the exercise of choice in education means that Americans have already lost freedom of mind and freedom of religion in the broad and important precincts of the education of the young.

Princeton's Dodds, like the Fathers of our nation, equates the freedom of our society with the freedom of the individual person. Society cannot be free unless its members are free. The basis of this freedom, moreover, is freedom of mind and spirit from government control. "The independent school in America," President Dodds declared, "is one of several voluntary, non-governmental and non-political islands of independence of thought and opinion indispensable in a society which is rapidly politicizing wide areas of life which not so long ago were the responsibilities of individuals and voluntary associations." [2]

These "voluntary, non-governmental and non-political islands of independence of thought and opinion"—the independent schools—must be defended against government aggression. A starvation policy against the occupiers of these islands, however, is as much governmental aggression as an open and frontal attack. This is the policy that demands the surrender of freedom of choice in education as a condition for sharing in education benefits. By these means government is forcing all children and students whose parents are unable to finance their education at an independent school to vacate these "islands of independence of thought and opinion" and to submit to government thought control.

This policy is destructive of the freedom of the individual; it is destructive of a free society. It destroys free enterprise in education; it will, if pursued, inevitably destroy free enterprise in our American economy. If present trends continue, it is estimated that by 1970 80 per cent of our college students will be registered in government-controlled institutions. In elementary and secondary education, the proportion in state schools will undoubtedly exceed 90 per cent. This means that the "voluntary, non-governmental and non-political islands of independence of thought and opinion" shall have been all but eliminated. Without such "islands" of freedom, how can freedom survive? Virtually all thought and opinion will be in government's control and grasp. What President Dodds calls "the right of the individual . . . to oppose and resist trends, political or educational, in favor of more traditional values which he believes to be more fundamental than the current taste of the numerical or political majority" [3] shall have been lost. All will be forced to conform in thought and belief to the decisions of the majority—decisions predetermined in this age of high-pressure propaganda by a relatively few individuals occupying positions of power or influence.

In discussing the merits of the certificate plan, Professor Thomson of the University of Chicago points up the importance of limiting the power of government in the field of education. "The fundamental rationale for transferring education from the public decision-making process to the private sphere," he writes, "is that it increases the freedom of choice of the individual or the family unit and reduces the authority of government." [4] The professor thereupon observes pointedly that "at a period of our history when every tendency seems destined to run in the opposite direction, this in itself is an achievement worthy of careful consideration." [5] In the final analysis the question that confronts America is this: Will government power continue to be partial or will it grow until it becomes total, that is, totalitarian?

When government draws more and more human activities into the orbit of its control, the area of the citizen's decision-making power is more and more circumscribed. Deprived of the right and opportunity to make decisions in important areas of human activities, man gradually loses his individuality and as he does so he becomes the mass man. The mass man, having lost his freedom of action, is in danger of becoming a moral non-entity. "Moral capacities must suffer where the ultimate decision of human welfare is released from the responsibility of the individual and transferred to government. . . . If the field of personal morality is reduced and that of government responsibility enlarged, it follows that the domain of personal value is narrowed by the increasing area of collective coercion," [6] writes Hans F. Sennholz in an essay on democracy.

And when government draws more and more human activities into the orbit of its control, the area of human activities in which the collective end replaces the personal ends of individuals is increasingly extended. When this happens, the stage is set for the tyranny of the majority—a majority that can run roughshod over the constitutional rights of individuals. And there is danger that it may do this with the Supreme Court's blessing, as was exemplified in the *Gobitis* decision. [7] "The very principle that the collective end is the sole end," reasons Professor Sennholz, "includes the principle that the collective end justifies all means. For the 'good of the whole' the individual must be prepared to sacrifice his own ends and apply every means necessary for the attainment of the common end. There is literally nothing that he must not be prepared to do. The collective end as understood by the leader [or the majority] is the sole criterion of what ought to be done. It is obvious that this system of collectivist morals violently contrasts with the morals of our civilization." [8] This is emphatically true. As the individual person is more and more submerged in the mass, his decision-making power is lost to the state and the morality of action becomes a question of collective morality. Professor Sennholz observes that "to exclude the consequences of our actions and means applied from our moral consideration and to limit our conscience to the consequences of the collective end is in fact to deny all morals." This is true, argues Sennholz, because "the individual in a collective society merely carries out orders; he is not free to act according to his own judgment and conviction." [9]

Growth of government power, including its expansive power over the mind and spirit, is what W. Homer Turner, executive director of the United States Steel Foundation, called, one of our major social diseases—"compulsory uniformity." This "excessive appetite for compulsory uniformity," observed Mr. Turner, is in part "related to the concept of the welfare state." [10] Enforced uniformity, though related to the concept of the welfare state, is not necessarily consequent upon this concept of the relationship of the individual and the state. It is true that the welfare state provides the apparatus for control and for compulsory uniformity, but a people dedicated to the principles of liberty will not clamp the mind and spirit of man into a strait-jacket simply because the opportunity is at hand.

If the American people are dedicated to freedom, they will be all the more alert to defend against its violation by government when the danger of such violations is increased by the growing apparatus of the welfare state. In the politics of state-controlled education there is, in the words of Mr. Turner, "a strong parallel movement to introduce a general uniformity into our educational life." [11] Though this problem has many facets, the fact is well exemplified by our American policy of enforced conformity to the philosophical and theological orientation of government schools as a condition for sharing in educational benefits.

A free society is not viable under conditions of compulsory uniformity. "A democratic society strangulates itself when it impairs the free trade in opinion and interest, political, social, economic, and cultural," writes Professor F. Morstein Marx. "Variety in these vital goods is strength, not weakness," [12] he continues.

There can be no free exchange of ideas, there can be no full and free discussion, when participation in the government's educational benefits is conditioned on the surrender of educational freedom—the freedom to exchange ideas and to pursue truth uninhibited by the strong arm of the state. This is the denial of academic freedom. "Discussion implies that there is more than one point of view. The notion that the truth is arrived at by discussion is peculiarly applicable to practical, political, economic matters," wrote Robert M. Hutchins in the *Saturday Review*.[13] But if government subsidizes the study of only some points of view and refuses to subsidize the study of other points of view, how can there be that freedom of discussion that is, particularly in practical matters, essential to the discovery of truth? Government, with its near limitless power, has, in the most fundamental of all issues—the philosophical and theological—entered the lists on the side of particular points of view. How then can truth prevail? Is not truth here determined by what President Dodds calls "the numerical or political majority"? The underlying philosophy of this unequal contest is that truth follows the party with the most votes, actual or manipulated. In other words might makes right. It is the philosophy of the absolute state.

For such a state of affairs, Mr. Hutchins has a severe indictment. He writes: "A civilization in which the opinion of the majority is taken on such matters and must then be adopted by all is one that is doomed to stagnation. It ignores the fact that the most precious right of any society is the thought of the minority, even a minority of one. The rule of the majority without discussion and criticism is tyranny." [14]

When government subsidizes the study and propagation of only one point of view in the most fundamental of all issues—philosophical and theological issues—how can truth in these matters prevail? Truth by itself cannot prevail against error if perchance the powers of government are aligned with error.

John Stuart Mill, the greatest exponent of freedom of discussion, declared: "It is a piece of idle sentimentality that truth, merely as truth, has an inherent power denied to error, of prevailing against the dungeon and the stake. Men are not more zealous for truth than they often are for error, and a sufficient application of legal or even of social penalties will generally succeed in stopping the propagation of either." [15]

For purposes of this discussion, the question of what philosophical system or what theological system contains the greater truth is irrelevant. The point is that in the American context of freedom, if truth is to prevail, government may not arbitrarily subsidize the study and propagation of any one system to the exclusion of all others. Yet this is precisely what American governments are doing. In the contest of truth and error, governments have entered their overwhelming financial resources in support of positivism and secularism. How unequal is the contest is well indicated by the progressive secularization of American society. In fact, "secularism has taken over in the United States," declared Methodist clergyman Paul Hutchinson.[16]

Put in another way, state educational policy, like the policy of secular education in general, is guilty of censorship—the censorship of selection. Dr. Francis M. Rogers, Harvard professor of romance languages and former dean of the Harvard graduate school, declared that the secular tradition of education allows itself "the luxury of all but ignoring great segments of knowledge: religion, theology, Catholicism." [17] But when education that pretends to treat of universal knowledge ignores great segments of knowledge, it is actually engaging in the grossest kind of censorship. "I believe it can be charged," Professor Rogers observed, "that the secular tradition, while protesting vigorously against censorship in any form, exercises a fierce kind of censorship, the censorship of selection, the selection involved in the organization of a course and a program of courses. Whole bodies of knowledge—useful, inter-esting, and beautiful knowledge—are often omitted en bloc. The impoverished student never knows the difference." [18]

But state educational policy can be charged with more than censorship, with more than the suppression of vast segments of knowledge in state-controlled educational institutions. By compelling the child and student to surrender their constitu-tional right of freedom of choice in education as a condition for sharing in educational benefits, the state is attempting to control their thought and belief. This is economic pressure brought to bear to achieve uniformity and conformity. This means in effect that truth is determined by majority vote and that children and students are forced to accept this definition of truth if they are to share in the educational benefits made available by the taxpayer. But a definition of truth by the state and enforced acceptance of that definition by students renders discussion, an exchange of ideas, and controversy about the most important issues of life virtually impossible. "A civiliza-tion in which there is not a continuous controversy about important issues, speculative and practical," warns Robert Hutchins, "is on the way to totalitarianism and death."

No one will maintain that in America there is full and free academic discussion of controverted basic ideas and issues. The discussion cannot be "full and free" when the exponents of one point of view go begging while the exponents of the other point of view are armed with the weapons secured by a multimillion dollar budget. Nonetheless, as Justice Douglas has said, "full and free discussion has indeed been the first article of our faith. We have founded our political system on it. . . . We have counted on it to keep us from embracing what is cheap and false; we have trusted the common sense of our people to choose the doctrine true to our genius and to reject the rest. This has been the one single outstanding tenet that has made our institutions the symbol of freedom and equality. . . . We have wanted a land where our people can be exposed to all the diverse creeds and cultures of the world." [19] Yet diversity is today being eradicated from our society; conformity is the prevailing doctrine. He who will not conform shall not share in the state's educational benefits.

The government that denies freedom of mind and freedom of spirit strangulates diversity. This destroys democracy. "The first distinctive feature of democracy," declared Rabbi Robert P. Jacobs of St. Louis, "is its cultural diversity." [20] Cultural diversity can be maintained only through diversity in education. Compulsory conformity in education is destructive of cultural diversity. Contrary to the statist philosophy of compulsory conformity, Rabbi Jacobs maintains that religion is "an outpost in the struggle for democracy." This Jewish leader rejects enforced conformity. He asserted: "Religion's role in the struggle for the maintenance and extension of democracy is . . . first of all to maintain and to extend the differentiation of a population which is itself an amalgamation of various nationality and religious groups. Democracy means the legal and moral right to preserve differences." [21]

The Rabbi's position is well based in constitutional principles. Within the guarantees of our Federal Constitution, democracy does not only mean the legal and moral right to preserve differences. It also means the legal and moral right to preserve these differences through the education of the young. Contrariwise, these rights deny to the state the power to use legal means or economic pressure to enforce conformity.

But religion is more than "an outpost in the struggle for democracy." It is the uniquely necessary defense against forces destructive of liberty and civilization. This is emphatically stated by Professor Samuel Eliot Morison of Harvard in his *Freedom in Contemporary Society*. He writes: "Only a Christian commonwealth is capable of preserving freedom; and without freedom nothing in what we call civilization is worth preserving." Moreover, he maintains that academic freedom or freedom in education "is but one of the many freedoms that come from God, who gave us our minds that we might rise a little nearer the angels; and without whose grace we are powerless for good." [22]

It seems to be a logical conclusion that if "only a Christian commonwealth is capable of preserving freedom," then the Christian religion must be transmitted from generation to generation. But this can be done effectively only through the prolonged process of formal education. If the profound principles of Christianity are to impregnate the heart and soul of the nation, they must be deeply embedded in the heart and mind of the vast majority of the citizens of our nation. This cannot be done through secularized education; it can be effectuated only if religion becomes an integral part of education.

Freedom of mind and freedom of spirit are essential ingredients of democracy. This fundamental principle has been repeatedly reasserted by judges of our highest judicial tribunal. Mr. Justice Holmes declared that "if there is any principle of the Constitution that more imperatively calls for attachment than any other it is the principle of free thought—not free thought for those who agree with us but freedom for the thought that we hate." [23] And Mr. Chief Justice Hughes asserted that "the essence of religion is belief in a relation to God involving duties superior to those arising from any human relation." [24] These convictions were re-emphasized by Mr. Justice Stone when he declared that "the Constitution expressed more than the conviction of the people that democratic processes must be preserved at all costs. It is also an expression of faith and a command that freedom of mind and spirit must be preserved, which government must obey, if it is to adhere to that justice and moderation without which no free government can exist." [25]

"Our real power," to repeat Mr. Justice Douglas, "is our spiritual strength, and that spiritual strength stems from our civil liberties. If we are true to our traditions, if we are tolerant of a whole market place of ideas, we will always be strong. Our weakness grows when we become intolerant of opposing ideas, depart from our standards of civil liberties, and borrow the policeman's philosophy from the enemy we detest." [26]

Liberty is fundamental to democracy. Democracy demands that the individual person be free, particularly in those things that determine what he shall think and what he shall believe. But this freedom of mind and freedom of religion cannot be achieved if children must conform to a particular kind of education as a condition for sharing in state educational benefits.

Freedom demands diversity. Freedom of thought demands diversity in the field of education. Diversity is the dominant characteristic of a pluralist society; enforced conformity is the dominant characteristic of an absolute state.

The absolute state is based on conformity. Enforced conformity in education leads inevitably to the kind of state in which there is and can be only *one* correct view—that is, the view adopted by the voting majority. All other views, whether in the area of free private enterprise, individual rights, minority rights, or private property are considered unorthodox, undemocratic, un-American, and intolerable. They must be suppressed.

Freedom demands diversity of organizations to achieve man's diverse purposes; it is incompatible with the absolute state that draws within its grasp all man's purposes and activities. Freedom demands that individuals be free to join voluntary associations for a variety of purposes, such as religious, cultural, educational, recreational, charitable, and economic.

Such a society creates a balance between the state and voluntary associations. Ernest Barker, as seen above, declares that this philosophy of liberty and government favors "the maximum of voluntary self-help by groups of individuals, voluntarily acting for themselves, in their own sphere of interest, the requirements and conditions of their own development; and, when they have thought them out *for* themselves, going on to achieve them *by* themselves, and by their own efforts, so far as in their own sphere they can." [27]

Professor Whitehead maintains that the modern method of solving the problem of liberty "consists in the deliberate formation of institutions, embodying purposes of special groups, and unconcerned with the general purposes of any political state." [28] Such autonomous associations will limit the power of the state; they will preserve the freedom of thought and action of the individual in important areas of human activity. Economic activities obviously fall within these areas. But Professor Barker points out that there are other fields in which the development of independent institutions "may contribute greatly to the solution of the ancient problem of liberty." This is the area of individual freedom of thought and freedom of religion. "There is, for example, the field of education, which is not, and never can be, a monopoly of the State. Educational associations—of parents, of teachers, of workers, and of members of religious confessions—are all concerned in the development of educational experiments, and in offering that liberty of choice among types of school and forms of instruction which is essential to the growth of personal and individual capacity." [29]

Where there is liberty, there is diversity. Where there is no diversity in voluntary institutions but only state monopoly, there liberty is curtailed, suppressed, and ultimately completely denied. Of all the areas of human activities that demand freedom from complete government control and domination, that of education is the most vital for the preservation of democracy. This is the area that touches the freedom of the human mind and spirit. The presence or absence of this freedom spells the difference between liberty and tyranny.

State educational policy that employs economic coercion to force children and students to conform to government educational philosophy not only violates the liberty and equal rights of the individual. It does more than that. It is by indirection forcing the limitation, if not the eradication, of voluntary educational institutions and bringing about state monopoly over the things of the mind and spirit. When this most fundamental freedom has been suppressed, it can be only a matter of time until all other voluntary associations will be eliminated and the state will exercise total control over all human activities. Such total control is of the essence of the totalitarian state.

# II

# Tax Relief Through
# Freedom of Choice
# in Education

*The certificate or tax credit plan makes possible considerable
savings for the taxpayer.*

Education is an expensive item. As we advance up the academic ladder, the cost of education mounts rapidly. On the
elementary and secondary levels, operating costs approximate,
as a national average, roughly $310 a year for each child in
our government schools. On the college level, the operating
expense per full-time student varies widely according to the
wide variation in function of the colleges and universities.

Tuition for in-state students attending state colleges and
universities is, on the average, about $150 a year. This in-
come provides for only a fraction of the actual cost of education. The difference between tuition and the actual cost of
education is, for the most part, paid by the taxpayer in the
form of local, state, and Federal grants. It is difficult to ascer-
tain the annual operating expense for the education of a student, but it is a fair estimate that the expense on the four-year
college and university level is, with exceptions, between $1,000
and $1,200 or more in 1958. The 1955 Maryland three-year-
old report on *The Needs of Higher Education in Maryland*
estimated that the cost was $1,000 per student.[1]

164

A California five-year-old study of 1953 reported that the operating expense per full-time student in the state colleges ranged from $1,376 in Humboldt State to $548 at San Jose State, and that the University range was from $1,429 at Santa Barbara to $5,636 at Davis.[2] In a 1957 study California estimated that the total 1970 operating expense, based on 1956 costs, for the education of 90,350 students on existing campuses would be $106,820,500, or $1,182 per student.[3]

In an effort to meet the inflated cost of education, independent colleges and universities have increased their tuition 50 to 100 per cent in the last ten years and have undertaken extensive fund-raising programs. The tuition increases in a few schools from 1947 to 1957 will indicate how rapidly the cost of education has gone up. Syracuse University raised its tuition from $450 to $900; Georgetown University from $450 to $850; Princeton University from $560 to $1,200; Johns Hopkins University from $500 to $1,000; and Radcliffe College from $450 to $1,000.[4]

Though the average American family would find considerable difficulty paying tuition charges at any of the above colleges and universities, these charges are more or less typical. And they do not include the cost of housing, board, fees, books, and incidentals. Yet these tuition charges do not begin to pay the actual operating expenses incurred by the universities and colleges. The *New York Times* survey of thirty-five well known and representative colleges and universities throughout the country found that "despite the substantial tuition increase, student fees cover only about *one-half* of the cost of a private college education. The rest of the expense has to be provided by the college from endowment, gifts and grants and other sources." [5]

The cost of supplying classroom and laboratory facilities for an ever-increasing number of children and students runs into astronomical figures. New elementary and secondary public schools in the boroughs of New York cost from $2,100 to $2,800 per child in 1957.[6] A special school, the High School of Industrial Art on Second Avenue and Fifty-seventh Street, was planned to accommodate 2,600 pupils and to cost $9,500,000 or $3,653 per pupil.[7] Construction costs in less populous areas are somewhat less.

On the college level the capital outlay for facilities is even more costly. In a plan proposing Federal aid for the construction of 400 public community *junior* colleges, Senator Clifford P. Case of New Jersey estimated the cost of the necessary facilities at $3,000 to $4,000 for each student.[8] For four-year colleges and universities the costs are considerably higher. In an effort to determine educational needs and costs on the higher level, California undertook an extensive study, which was completed in 1957. The report gives the estimated capital outlay per student, at 1956 costs, for the expansion of the University of California's teaching campuses to 1970. The estimates represent 78.5 per cent of cost which is approximately the state's share in University capital outlay. State's share (78.5 per cent of actual cost) of capital outlay at Berkeley, UCLA, and Davis is estimated at $5,000 per student; Santa Barbara and Riverside at $4,825 per student; San Diego at $4,825 per Liberal Arts student and $10,000,000 additional for science and technology expansion; San Francisco Medical Center at $10,000 per student; southeast Los Angeles estimated at $8,545 per student; Santa Clara Valley at $8,782 per student.[9] But the estimated expense per student in the projection of the State College system to 1970 is approximately $4,000.[10]

It is estimated, moreover, that about one-fourth of the student body of a college will require dormitory accommodations. The variables that determine the actual cost of dormitory construction are many, but a reasonable estimate for such accommodations is $3,800 per student.[11]

In view of the high cost of state education, the taxpayer is understandably interested in the answers to some fundamental questions. Will the state's virtual monopoly in education on the elementary and secondary levels necessitate an ever-increasing tax burden to provide for the education needs of an ever-increasing number of school-age children? Will the increase of more than 4,000,000 college students by 1970 be assimilated by both government and independent colleges, or almost exclusively by government educational institutions at ever-increasing cost to the taxpayer?

In 1957–1958 there are an estimated 39,000,000 children attending elementary and secondary schools in America. From 1956–1957 to 1957–1958 the enrollment on the elementary and secondary levels increased by more than 1,500,000.[12] If this increase for a single year is projected to 1970, twelve years beyond the present, it is expected that the school-age population (age 5 to 17) will be 57,000,000.

Of the estimated 39,000,000 school children of 1957–1958, 5,408,000 (about 14 per cent) are enrolled in independent schools and 33,392,000 in public schools.[13] If 14 per cent of the projected school population of 1970 attend independent schools, there will be 7,980,000 in attendance at such schools and 49,020,000 in government schools. This represents an increase in government schools of 15,628,000 and in independent schools of 2,572,000 by 1970.

These figures would seem to indicate that the public school system will have to provide facilities for 15,628,000 additional children. Moreover, it seems that the public-school system will have to provide teachers for a total of 49,020,000 children on the elementary and secondary levels of education by 1970.

If it is assumed that operating expenses will not rise considerably above $340 per child by 1970, what will be the operating expenses of the government schools of the nation?[14] And if it is assumed that capital outlay is $1,800 per child in government schools (a conservative figure when compared with the New York estimates given above), what will be the total sum required to supply facilities for more than 15,000,000 additional children by 1970?

If it is assumed that only 14 per cent of the school-age children will be attending independent schools, the taxpayer will have to pay the operating expenses for the public school education of 49,020,000 pupils by 1970. At $340 per child, this will cost the taxpayer $16,666,800,000 annually. And if, moreover, it is assumed that 86 per cent of our children will continue to attend government schools by 1970, the taxpayer will have to supply facilities for an additional 15,628,000 children. At $1,800 per pupil, this will involve a capital outlay of no less than $28,130,400,000. This does not include the replacement cost of old and dilapidated buildings.

The adoption of the certificate or tax credit plan would involve savings for the taxpayer that run into billions of dollars on the elementary and secondary levels of education alone.

It is impossible to conjecture how many parents would send their children to independent schools if the several states and/or the Federal Government adopted the certificate or tax credit plan. But if it is assumed that 25 per cent would exercise their new-won freedom of choice in education and send their children to independent schools, what would be the saving for the taxpayer in capital-outlay expenditures and in annual operating expenses? This depends in large measure on the size of the subsidy granted to parents or guardians for the education of the individual child in the school of their choice. How large should the subsidy be? It is difficult to determine what would be an equitable subsidy for the education of the child whose parents elect to send him to an independent school. Prescinding from the question of equity, it would, no doubt, be instructive and of interest to parents and taxpayers alike to investigate the probable results of the adoption of a certificate or tax credit plan providing a subsidy of $150 for the education of each child attending an independent school.

If it is assumed that 25 per cent of our school-age children would, under the certificate or tax credit plan, attend independent schools, there would be 14,250,000 children attending such schools by 1970. This would result in public school attendance of 42,750,000. This is 6,270,000 fewer than the 49,020,000 projected for 1970 if only 14 per cent of our children attend independent schools. For the taxpayer, this would constitute tremendous savings in capital outlay and substantial annual savings in operational costs.

The cost of providing facilities for each child is, as seen above, about $1,800. If the taxpayer were relieved of the burden of capital outlay involved in supplying facilities for 6,270,000 children, this would constitute a saving, directly consequent upon the adoption of the certificate or tax credit plan, of no less than $11,286,000,000 by 1970.

The operating expenses, at $340 per child, for 49,020,000 (86 per cent of the projected 1970 school-age group) will be $16,666,800,000 annually. For 42,750,000 children (75 per cent of the projected 1970 school-age group) the operating expenses would be reduced to $14,535,000,000 annually. This would constitute a yearly saving in operational costs of $2,131,800,000.

But this saving would be largely consumed in the granting of certificates or tax credits of $150 to parents for the education of each child going to an independent school. If parents of 25 per cent of our school-age children exercised freedom of choice in sending their children to independent schools, the parents of 14,250,000 children would qualify as recipients of certificates or tax credits to help them pay tuition for the education of their children. This would involve annual government subsidies, direct or indirect, to parents of independent-school children of $2,037,500,000. If this figure is subtracted from the amount saved in the operating expenses of government schools, the annual saving in current educational costs, even while subsidizing the education of all children, would be $94,300,000.

In a word, the adoption of the certificate or tax credit plan to give parents of elementary and secondary school children freedom of choice in education would give the American taxpayer considerable relief. The annual relief by 1970 would be only $94,300,000, but the relief enjoyed in expenditures for additional school facilities would reach the very substantial figure of $11,286,000,000 by 1970.

The progressive centralization of education on the college level in the hands of government has been even more costly for the taxpayer. The rapid shift of students from independent to public colleges and universities has made the taxpayer acutely and painfully aware of the growing imbalance between government and independent education. As recently as 1951 more than 50 per cent of our college students were registered in independent educational institutions. In that year 1,064,450 students, or 50.3 per cent, were in independent institutions and 1,051,990, or 49.7 per cent, were enrolled in public colleges and universities. By 1956 the trend toward public education had become very pronounced. Registration in independent institutions had decreased to 42.9 per cent, or 1,265,314 students. Enrollment in public institutions had risen sharply to 57.1 per cent, or 1,681,671 students.[15]

The trend toward government education is emphasized by the fact that in total enrollment of degree-credit students, government institutions reported an increase of 12.2 per cent in the fall of 1956 over the preceding fall, as compared with a 7.2 per cent rise in independent institutions.[16]

In Michigan the proportion of students in independent institutions is as low as 16 per cent; in California as low as 20 per cent. It has been estimated that by 1970 the across-the-nation proportion of the students in government institutions will reach 80 per cent.[17]

It is projected that by 1970 the college-age group—from 18 to 21—will contain from 13,610,000 to 14,278,000 persons. Experts disagree as to what per cent of these young men and women will seek admission to college. Some experts maintain that by 1970 the number of college students will reach 6,000,000; others say that this figure is too conservative, that it may be as high as 8,000,000 or more. And President Francis H. Horn of Pratt Institute predicted that the number of college students would rise to 9,000,000 by 1970.[18]

If it is assumed conservatively that by 1970 there will be 7,000,000 qualified young men and women admitted to higher educational institutions, what will this mean to the taxpayer in terms of dollars and cents? If 80 per cent of the projected number of students will be admitted to state institutions, there will be 5,600,000 students in such schools. If this happens, the several states shall have to provide educational facilities and accommodations for an additional 3,918,000 students by 1970. This is in addition to the 1,682,000 registered in government institutions in 1956–1957.

The cost of providing facilities for college-level students varies considerably, as indicated above. If the conservative figure of $3,500 per student is used, a rough estimate of the cost of supplying facilities for additional students can be ascertained.

To provide facilities for the projected increase of 3,918,000 students by 1970 (80 per cent of the total increase) at $3,500 per student would cost the fantastic sum of $13,713,000,000. This is equivalent to $80 for every man, woman, and child in the United States.

It is estimated, moreover, that about one-fourth of the student body of higher educational institutions will require dormitory accommodations. To house one-fourth of the increase in public institutions (979,500) would cost, at $3,800 per student, an additional $3,722,100,000 subject to amortization. This amounts to a total capital outlay of $17,435,100,-000 to provide educational facilities and dormitory accommodations for those students who shall reach state institutions of higher education by 1970.

The operating expenses involved in the education of 80 per cent of the projected student group by 1970 will rise rapidly. When the President's Committee on Education Beyond the High School recommended that faculty salaries be doubled within five to ten years,[19] it was reflecting the prevailing thought on the subject. There can, in fact, be little doubt that faculty salaries will be substantially increased in the years to come. This will result in sharp increases in operating costs per student. But if, for the sake of calculations, we project to 1970 the very conservative operating costs of $1,170 per student, thus reflecting very little of the anticipated increase in operational expenses, what will be the cost to the taxpayer if 80 per cent of the projected students shall be registered in state-controlled institutions? If we subtract from the per student operating costs a tuition charge of $170 per student, thus reflecting a conservative increase,[20] the cost to the taxpayer for each student will be $1,000 per year. The cost for the education of 5,600,000, or 80 per cent of the anticipated student enrollment for 1970, will thus be $5,600,000,000 annually.

What would be the impact on the taxpayer if the progressive socialization of education on the college level were halted and even reversed by the adoption of the certificate or tax credit plan? Since the single most important factor in the student's choice of a state institution over an independent institution is the low tuition, a substantial state subsidy to students to enable them to pay in part tuition at the school of their choice would, there can be little doubt, induce many young men and women to go to independent schools who must now, for financial reasons, attend government institutions.

It is difficult to determine what would be an equitable subsidy for the college student who exercises his constitutional right in the choice of an independent educational institution. (It should be noted that students who leave their home state to pursue their studies in public institutions of other states would, under any state certificate or tax credit plan, obviously be entitled to the same subsidy as are students pursuing their studies in independent colleges and universities. All students, whether in state or independent colleges, would likewise participate in Federal certificate or tax credit plans.) Prescinding from the question of equity, what would be the saving enjoyed by the taxpayer if the several states (or the Federal Government) adopted a certificate or tax credit plan which provided a subsidy of $500 a year to students attending independent institutions and if 50 per cent of the students projected for 1970, exercising freedom of choice in education, decided to attend independent colleges and universities?

If 50 per cent of the students projected for 1970 elected to attend independent institutions, 3,500,000 would attend such schools, and 3,500,000 would attend government colleges and universities.

This would amount to an increase in public institutions of 1,818,000 over the 1956 enrollment of 1,682,000. It would mean an increase of 2,235,000 in independent institutions which, in 1956, enrolled 1,265,000 students.

If 80 per cent of our college students will be attending government institutions by 1970, the several states will have to supply additional facilities for 3,918,000 young men and women. This would cost $13,713,000,000 in capital outlay. But if, under the certificate or tax credit plan, state institutions enrolled only 50 per cent of the students projected for

1970 (3,500,000), additional facilities would have to be provided for only 1,818,000 students. This would cost $6,363,-000,000 in capital outlay. If such were the result of the adoption of the certificate or tax credit plan, the saving enjoyed by the taxpayer would be very substantial. The saving by 1970 would be no less than $7,350,000,000 in capital outlay.

If 80 per cent of our college students will be attending public institutions by 1970, the several states will have to supply dormitory accommodations for 979,500 students at a cost of $3,722,100,000 subject to amortization. But if only 50 per cent of our students attend government institutions, the states will have to supply accommodations for 454,500 students at a cost of $1,727,100,000 subject to amortization. The saving enjoyed by 1970 would be $1,995,000,000.

If 80 per cent of our college students will be attending government institutions by 1970, the operational costs to the taxpayer for the education of 5,600,000 students, at $1,000 per student, will be $5,600,000,000 annually. But if only 50 per cent of our students attend state institutions of higher learning, the operational costs will be $3,500,000,000 annually. This would constitute a saving to the taxpayer in operating expenses of $2,100,000,000 yearly. But this saving would be largely consumed by government subsidies, direct or indirect, given to the 50 per cent of our students enrolled in independent educational institutions.

Subsidies, in certificates or tax credits, of $500 to each of 3,500,000 students to enable them to pay in part the tuition in the school of their choice would cost $1,750,000,000 annually. If this is deducted from the saving incurred in the operating costs of our government colleges and universities, a saving of $350,000,000 annually would still be enjoyed by the taxpayer.

In a word, the adoption of the certificate or tax credit plan to assist students to pay tuition in the schools of their choice would, if 50 per cent of them took advantage of the program by 1970, give the taxpayer substantial relief. The relief by 1970 for operating expenses would be $350,000,000 annually. In capital outlay for dormitory accommodations, the taxpayer would be saved $1,995,000,000 subject to amortization. In capital outlay for general facilities, the taxpayer would be saved $7,350,000,000. Independent institutions would, of course, spend an increasing amount to improve and enlarge their facilities.

There can be no doubt that the adoption of the certificate or tax credit plan to enable both children and college students to pay in part tuition at the school of their choice would result in very substantial savings for the taxpayer. If it is assumed that by 1970 the parents of 25 per cent of our children and 50 per cent of our students exercised their new-won freedom of mind and spirit in the choice of independent schools, the taxpayer would be saved $444,300,000 annually even while subsidizing directly or indirectly the education of every child and every student in the United States. In capital outlay for general facilities, excluding dormitories, he would be saved $18,-636,000,000.

Although it is apparent that the plan would effect a considerable saving for the taxpayer, yet it should not be forgotten that the weightiest reasons in support of the plan are not the tax savings involved but the fact that it enables government to assist every child and student to pursue knowledge and truth regardless of his exercise of freedom of mind or freedom of religion in the choice of school. No child or student would be denied educational benefits because of his exercise of a constitutional right in the choice of school.

# 12

# Effects of Freedom of
# Choice on Independent
# Higher Education

*The certificate or tax credit plan would, as an incidental re-*
*sult, enable independent colleges to raise their tuition to*
*something approximating the cost of education and thus be*
*better enabled to fulfill their essential function in our democ-*
*racy.*

"What most protects freedom of choice in America is the
great diversity of its institutions, none of which possesses overriding power. . . . Human beings and their institutions being
what they are, total power is not safe in the hand of any single
group no matter how well intentioned," declared the Commission on Financing Higher Education.[1]

It may be assumed that most Americans agree with the
Commission that a diversity of educational institutions is
necessary for the preservation of liberty. One of the major
educational problems that confront America today is to secure
the preservation of this diversity in education. If diversity in
education is to be preserved, the independent colleges and
universities must find ways and means to balance their budgets
and to improve their academic operations. The budgetary
problems of our 661 state educational institutions, though by
no means non-existent, are small when compared with the

financial difficulties that threaten the survival of a large majority of our 1,225 independent institutions.[2]

When speaking about the financial difficulties of independent schools, it is unrealistic to lump all such institutions together on the assumption that the problems facing them are identical or of equal magnitude. The problem for a small number of independent institutions is merely one of improving an already well-integrated, well-financed, highly endowed educational operation. The problem for many hundreds of other independent institutions, on the other hand, critically touches every phase of the educational activity at its very heart: faculty salaries, faculty quality, research facilities, research funds, classroom space, scholarship funds, library acquisitions and plant funds. No school can perform its true educational function if it is forever fighting for mere survival. And no school that is constantly fighting for mere survival is in a position to compete in the educational market place for faculty additions, for scholarship funds, for the best-qualified students, for corporation and private gifts, or for grants from the hundreds of foundations and from the Federal Government.

This condition brings about a kind of vicious circle. The more funds a school has, whether by reason of direct government subsidization or by reason of a large endowment, the easier it is for the school to obtain additional funds. This condition widens the gap between the endowed schools and the unendowed schools. While the relative position of these latter schools grows continually worse, the position of the tax-supported and highly endowed institutions of higher learning improves continually.

The consequences of this state of affairs are highly injurious to the proper education of American youth. The following conditions are found more or less universally in the unendowed independent institutions: (1) salary schedules fail to keep pace with schedules in other schools and in industry and, as a result, the best teachers are frequently lost; (2) low salaries make it more and more difficult to attract new faculty members; (3) general low salary scales induce trained personnel to enter industry rather than teaching, thus heightening the teacher shortage; (4) scientific laboratory equipment grows out of date and is not replaced; (5) new equipment to keep abreast of new developments cannot be purchased; (6) potential scholars refuse teaching positions because of inadequate research facilities; (7) budding scholars leave the academic life because the school is incapable of giving its faculty the time and leisure to do research; (8) library acquisitions are below basic academic requirements; (9) well qualified students fail to go to college because the local independent college has insufficient scholarships to provide for needy students; (10) classroom facilities deteriorate and cannot be replaced; (11) enrollment cannot be substantially increased because of a lack of plant funds for additional buildings; and (12) library facilities are inadequate for current enrollment, to say nothing of accommodating additional students.

The weak academic position of a large majority of independent colleges and universities is aggravated by the large budgets of state and highly endowed independent institutions of higher learning. This is consequent upon the fact that some of the most important aspects of education are competitive. The more state funds are appropriated for public institutions, the more difficult the situation becomes for independent institutions generally. The more foundation funds are given to public and selected independent institutions, the more difficult it becomes for the unendowed institutions. The more Federal funds are granted to public and selected independent institutions, the more difficult it becomes for the unendowed institutions. The more private and corporation funds are channeled into public and selected independent institutions, the more difficult it becomes for the unendowed institutions.

Present approaches to the financial problems of educational institutions do very little, at best, to enable the typical independent school to remedy these serious conditions. Although vast amounts of money are being appropriated for education and research in state and independent institutions by state governments, the Federal Government, foundations, corporations, and private individuals, the financial problems of the majority both of independent universities and of colleges are not being alleviated—they are thereby being aggravated.

The results of present policies are indicated by the increasing concentration of strength in physical plant in a relatively small group of institutions. The top strongest 37 institutions (2 per cent of all institutions) reported plant worth of $2,373,-197,604, or 31.4 per cent of the nation-wide total of $7,559,-555,820 in 1954. This means that 2 per cent of the institutions of the nation had more than 30 per cent of the plant. Further analysis of the 1954 data shows that the largest 19 institutions (1 per cent of the total number) held just over 21 per cent of the total plant and equipment. Of these 19 institutions, 13 were publicly controlled; of the 6 under independent control, 2 received some state or Federal funds.[3]

State and local appropriations for current expenses in higher education in 1953–1954 were $839,754,109. (During that year Federal grants to state colleges and universities for research reached $113,832,989, and other appropriations and grants reached about $40,000,000.)[4] In the same year state and local governments appropriated $155,232,571 for the purpose of purchasing new sites, construction or major remodeling of buildings, purchase of equipment, and other items tending to increase the physical holdings of educational institutions.[5]

These funds for the education of American youth in no way help toward the education of those young men and women who have elected to attend independent institutions. This denial of an educational subsidy forces independent schools to subsidize these students to the extent of half the cost of education. Here lies the source of most of the major problems of these institutions.

The vicious-circle paradox of the availability of funds to educational institutions which, relatively speaking, are well-financed is exemplified by Federal Government grants. Colleges and universities with quality faculties and research facilities and leisure receive research grants that pay for a large portion of their research programs. Colleges and even large universities that cannot, for lack of funds, meet these requirements of faculty and facilities generally receive a categorical refusal when they apply for Federal grants.

A total of $383,554,973 was contributed to higher education by the Federal Government in 1953–1954. Of this amount, $8,380,040 (2 per cent) was for plant expansion and $375,-174,933 (98 per cent) for current purposes. Federal grants to land-grant colleges came to $50,551,637. And $42,244,218 went for tuition and other costs paid by the Federal Government for training programs under the Department of Defense, and other miscellaneous items.[6]

Federal grants for research amounted to $282,379,078 in 1953–1954. Of this amount, $113,832,989 (40 per cent) was granted to state institutions and $168,546,089 (60 per cent) to independent institutions. More than three-fourths (77 per cent) went to universities, the payments being divided with almost complete equality between those under public control and those under independent control. State universities received $108,380,094 and independent universities received virtually the same amount, $108,972,332.[7]

Another 20.7 per cent of the Federal grants went to technological schools, chiefly to institutions under independent control. Public institutions received $2,225,849; independent schools received $56,167,557. The remaining 2.3 per cent went to liberal arts colleges, teachers colleges, other professional schools, and junior colleges. Liberal arts colleges, numerous though they are, received grants to the amount of $3,916,209. Of these grants colleges under government control received $1,494,401, and the hundreds of colleges under independent control received only $2,421,808.[8]

The United States Office of Education survey of Statistics of Higher Education, which breaks down the distribution of these Federal grants by regions and states, shows that the institutions receiving the largest Federal grants are located in Massachusetts, New York, Pennsylvania, Illinois, Michigan, Maryland, and California, and that the institutions receiving grants beyond comparison with other institutions are, in every state excepting Michigan, independent schools. These states are, of course, the homes of the "big name" independent universities.[9] The ordinary universities and the liberal arts colleges do not share, save by way of exception, in the Federal Government contracts and grants.

The Federal Government "is currently expending well over a billion dollars a year in activities which have a direct impact on education beyond the high school," declared the President's Committee on Education Beyond the High School. Of this amount, roughly between $350,000,000 and $450,000,000 is granted to colleges and universities on the basis of research contracts and grants.[10] Although these contracts and grants may not cover the actual cost of the research projects, yet they constitute for many colleges and universities an essential support for their research programs.

How essential such support is becomes apparent when the Federal proportion of the costs of such programs is revealed. The President's Committee reported that "it is estimated that over half of the total annual expenditures for research at colleges and universities throughout the Nation now comes from

Federal agencies. In some fields, such as physics, the Federal proportion is closer to 90 per cent." [11]

For colleges and universities which receive Federal contracts and grants, the Federal subsidy program has become a major factor in research programs. "Hundreds of scientists and thousands of graduate students," says the President's Committee, "are now being supported, in whole or in part, by Federal funds. A survey of 32 leading colleges and universities made in 1952 reported that 14,000 people on their staffs were employed full-time or part-time on Government research, and that the percentage of Government contract employees in these institutions ranged from a low of 1 per cent to more than 50 per cent." [12]

This vast outpouring of Federal funds into a small number of colleges and universities not only worsens the relative position of other colleges and universities, but this government policy makes it extremely difficult for potentially good science departments in other colleges and universities to inaugurate a serious research program. They need funds to get their program under way; but they can't get funds from the government because their program is not under way. The President's Committee reports that "there has been complaint that the contracts have been too much concentrated, with the result that a few outstanding institutions have received a disproportionate share of research contracts and research personnel." [13]

The Federal Government's policy in giving contracts and grants has certain consequences in institutional life. First, schools that have been favored with Federal grants have been enabled to expand their research programs and to acquire expensive laboratory equipment. This makes it possible for these institutions to hire hundreds of the best research scholars, many of them from other institutions, and to grant substantial research fellowships to hundreds of graduate students.

Secondly, these Federal grants, since education is in many aspects competitive, have made it considerably more difficult for colleges which do not qualify for such grants to hire well-trained faculty members. Federal research programs have not turned out a large number of newly trained teachers, yet they have assimilated many hundreds of our best-qualified professors. The secondary result of this drainage of good teachers from the typical college is the consequent failure of these colleges to produce good undergraduate students—students who might, if properly trained, continue in graduate work and advance to the doctoral degree. Thus the ultimate result of this Federal grant program may well be the deterioration of scientific teaching in the majority of our colleges, and the consequent lowering of scientific learning in our nation.

All this is not to intimate that the Federal Government should not make grants to schools that are best equipped to provide the service the several government agencies demand. Nevertheless, it seems to be a fact that current Federal policy for research helps to accentuate the vast disparity between funds available to state and selected independent schools, on the one hand, and the funds available to independent schools in general, on the other hand. And this disparity, as already shown, aggravates the problems of these independent institutions.

American foundations control about $7,200,000,000 in funds. During 1956 these foundations made grants amounting to about $600,000,000. Foundations are made possible by provisions in tax laws. Gifts to them enjoy tax deductibility by the donors. The income from the investment of such gifts, moreover, is given tax exemption by both Federal and state laws.[14] The tax deductibility and tax exemption that these foundations enjoy gives the public a definite interest in how these funds are used. It might, therefore, be assumed that foundations whose purpose is to assist education, scholarship, and research would make grants on an extensive rather than intensive basis. But this has not been the case. With the exception of a few foundations, such as the Ford Foundation and the United States Steel Foundation, foundations seem, for the most part, to be pouring their money into a relatively small number of selected colleges and universities.

Former President Herbert Hoover declared in a letter to the Council for the Advancement of Small Colleges that the failure of the great foundations to support small colleges "is the greatest gap in their otherwise great contribution to American education." [15] Mr. Hoover feels that small colleges particularly deserve financial assistance because of the high purpose they serve. He continues: "These colleges are close to the people. They have served our people for long years through dedicated and self-denying teachers. Their intimate relations with the students enable them to do a better job in character-building than our great institutions with their high attendance." [16]

The students of these colleges generally come from the immediate locality and are, in large part, unable to meet the cost of education away from home. These small colleges are going concerns. They serve a good purpose in the nation's educational effort. "They represent an already-invested capital of $65,000,000 and they are providing for about 25,000 students," wrote Hoover. Furthermore, continued the former President, "we are short of higher educational facilities in every state for enlargement of mind and professional training, and students are being turned away every autumn. To put these small colleges on their feet would probably cost less than $75,000,000 which is probably not 10 per cent of the annual gifts to the larger institutions." [17]

What Dr. K. Duane Hurley, president of the Council for the Advancement of Small Colleges, said about the plight of the colleges lacking accreditation is equally true in another sense of most independent educational institutions. Dr. Hurley called attention to what is, in fact, a vicious circle—"you need accreditation to get money and money to get accreditation." [18]

Certainly it can be said that the vast majority of independent educational institutions find themselves in the same predicament in their efforts to secure foundation funds. They need a high-quality faculty and research facilities to get funds and funds to get a high-quality faculty and research facilities.

A glance at foundation grants to one particular group of independent colleges and universities will show to what extent foundations, based on general tax concessions, are failing to assist education in general. During 1955 and 1956 American foundations made grants amounting to well over $1,000,000,-000. In January, 1957, 254 Catholic colleges and universities were asked to report foundation grants received during 1955 and 1956. Only 107 institutions answered the questionnaire sent out by the National Catholic Educational Association. Of this number, 20 institutions reported that they had received no foundation grants in that period. It may reasonably be conjectured that the vast majority of the 147 institutions which failed to answer the questionnaire received no substantial grants save the Ford Foundation grants.[19]

The 107 reporting institutions received a total of $23,534,-103 in 615 grants during the years 1955 and 1956. Of this total, the Ford Foundation (or its subsidiary foundations) gave $17,415,236, or 74 per cent. This means that in two years all other foundations gave the 107 reporting Catholic colleges and universities only $6,118,867.[20] This averages out to about $28,500 a year to each of the 107 Catholic institutions of higher learning, many of which are large universities and have been serving the nation and particular communities for the greater part of a century.

It should be pointed out that in 1956 the Ford Foundation

was making its generous grants to all accredited institutions, both denominational and nondenominational. These grants, not likely to be repeated, were quite substantial. However, over 75 per cent of the grants received by the 107 reporting Catholic institutions of higher education were less than $5,000 each, and about one-third of them $1,000 or less.[21]

Private donations to higher education amounted to $418,-468,653 in 1953–1954. This figure includes gifts and grants of more than $191,000,000 for current educational and general purposes, nearly $17,000,000 for student aid, almost $104,-000,000 for plant expansion, and well over $106,000,000 for increase of permanent funds.[22]

Gifts to independent institutions ($345,333,749) outnumbered those to state institutions ($73,134,904) by nearly 5 to 1. Universities received 49.6 per cent of the total of all gifts and liberal arts colleges 32.5 per cent. The remaining 17.9 per cent was scattered among the five other groups in varying amounts.[23]

The pattern of gift-giving in the past is demonstrated by the concentration of endowment funds in a relatively small number of institutions. While a small number of institutions have very large endowments, almost half of all colleges and universities have no endowment whatsoever. Permanent funds or endowment funds reached the astronomical figure of $3,196,120,125 in 1954. In addition to these funds educational institutions held student loan funds amounting to $49,192,177 and funds subject to annuity agreements amounting to $67,252,717. Yet, 805, or 43 per cent, of the 1871 institutions, enrolling 25 per cent of the resident students of college grade in November, 1953, had *no* endowment funds of any type.[24]

A limited number of institutions had a very large percentage of the endowment of all higher education in 1954.

A count of institutions with the largest endowment funds shows that 18 (1 per cent of the total number) had just under 45 per cent of the national total. This list includes 4 institutions under public control and 14 under the control of the churches and other philanthropic or altruistic organizations.[25]

Moreover, twenty-three institutions, which constituted 1.23 per cent, or just under one-eightieth of the number of institutions, had a total of 49.82 per cent of the endowment, or almost exactly one-half of it. The 38 institutions in the Boston Metropolitan area had 10.91 per cent of the endowment funds of all higher education in the nation. The two states of Massachusetts and New York had just over 25 per cent of the total endowment funds of all higher education in the nation. And in at least one state (Michigan) the State University had more endowment funds than all the other 54 institutions of higher education in the state.[26]

When all assets, permanent and quasi-permanent, are considered, it appears that no fewer than 29 institutions have assets of these 2 types amounting to $50,000,000 or more per institution. This group of institutions includes 20 under government control and 19 under the control of independent organizations. The total of the assets of the entire group of 39 institutions comes to a little under $4,250,000,000 and comprises 37 per cent of the total of $11,345,265,359 held by all institutions in the nation. Further analysis shows that 25.9 per cent of the national total of all permanent or quasi-permanent assets of higher education is held by 1 per cent of the institutions. Even more striking is the fact that more than 10 per cent is held by 4 institutions, of which 2 are public and 2 are independent.[27]

Another substantial source of income for selected independent universities and colleges is the earnings of endowment and other nonexpendable funds. Such earnings amounted to

$127,533,025 in 1953–1954. Of this total, state institutions reported $14,704,050, or 11.5 per cent, and independent institutions reported $112,828,975, or 88.5 per cent.[28]

Gift-giving for current expenses has followed the same pattern; a few prestige colleges and universities receive a very large proportion of such gifts, while the vast majority of institutions receive relatively small benefactions. For every student registered at an institution of higher education in 1953–1954, private gifts and grants for current purposes amounting to $76.15 were received. These contributions ran highest in the Northeastern areas ($90.93 per student) and the North Central areas ($89.59), and the lowest in the West ($45.24). They averaged more than $140 per student in New Hampshire, Connecticut, and Massachusetts, the home states of Dartmouth, Yale, and Harvard, respectively.[29]

The American Alumni Council, with a membership of "807 leading colleges and universities," reported that in 1956 college alumni gave their institutions a total of $102,000,000. It also reported that colleges and universities received gifts from "all sources" amounting to about $500,000,000. A comparative analysis of the lists of institutions in the two groups reveals that nine of the ten schools which lead in alumni gifts also lead in gifts from all sources: [30]

| *Alumni gifts* | | *Total gifts, all sources* | |
|---|---|---|---|
| Yale | $11,286,607 | Yale | $23,510,925 |
| Harvard | 9,238,619 | N.Y. Univ. | 14,283,541 |
| M.I.T. | 4,223,950 | Stanford | 10,674,368 |
| Wellesley | 2,251,638 | Cornell | 10,436,540 |
| Dartmouth | 2,166,944 | M.I.T. | 10,387,000 |
| N.Y. Univ. | 1,865,929 | Harvard | 9,715,165 |
| Princeton | 1,818,142 | Columbia | 7,470,742 |
| Columbia | 1,633,423 | Princeton | 6,012,425 |
| Stanford | 1,209,704 | Dartmouth | 4,432,207 |
| Cornell | 1,132,817 | Western Res. | 4,267,234 |

The same *nine* institutions received more than *one-third* ($34,576,133) of all alumni gifts and about *one-fifth* of all gifts from all sources ($96,922,913) given to "807 leading colleges and universities."

The same pattern of gift-giving was reported for 1956–1957 in a survey by the John Price Jones Company fund-raising organization. This survey, covering fifty colleges and universities, shows that these institutions had received $272,-734,000 in gifts and bequests from *private sources*. This figure represents a 30.3 per cent increase over the previous year's high of $209,274,000. Since 1950–1951, it might be pointed out, these fifty institutions have received in gifts and bequests $1,106,188,000.

Although these fifty colleges and universities are undoubtedly among the nation's leading educational institutions in terms of contributions received, it should be noted that *seven* of their number received exactly half, or $136,240,000, of the total received in gifts and bequests. Harvard received $22,559,-000; Yale, $20,793,000; Stanford, $20,836,000; Columbia, $19,086,000; Chicago, $18,182,000; Cornell, $17,836,000, and Johns Hopkins, $17,288,000.[31]

The extent of alumni giving is not simply a measure of loyalty to Alma Mater. It is also a measure of income, family status, business, and professional connections. Both of the latter are generally possessed by a large proportion of students who attend the "big name" high-tuition institutions. On graduation these young men and women frequently are able to enter a business or professional career as junior members of a prospering firm. They are not the first in their family to receive the advantages of higher education. As a consequence alumni of such colleges and universities are generally in a position to give generously to the school they attend.

Students who attend the small low-tuition independent liberal arts colleges or the low-tuition independent universities in our metropolitan areas, on the other hand, generally come from low-income families with little or no significant business or professional connections. The income of alumni with such a background will generally be measurably lower than that of graduates who have entered a business or professional career as a junior partner of a going concern. With a lower income such alumni not only have less to give to their Alma Mater, but the tax inducements to such giving are also, consequently, considerably less.

Another factor in alumni giving that should at least be noted is that the hand-to-mouth existence of many hundreds of small colleges makes it impossible for them to budget funds for the organizational apparatus, continuous campaigning and personal contact that are essential for effective alumni solicitation. As a consequence the per cent of living alumni contributing is very low and the average gift contributed is very small.

A source of income that is substantially higher in the "big name" colleges and universities than in the typical institution is tuition. Tuition in most of the former schools runs between $900 and $1,200 a year, while the charge in most of the non-prestige colleges and universities is between $300 and $700. These low tuition charges are fixed by the economic facts of life. These schools are in direct competition with low-tuition state institutions. Consequently, the administration of these independent schools must determine the point of diminishing returns—the point at which economic factors will force so many potential students to attend state institutions that an increase in tuition will result in a worsening of the school's financial conditions.

Dr. B. Garrison Lipton, writing to the *New York Times*, gives a convincing answer to the proposal calling for student payment of the entire cost of his education. He writes: "Dr. Seymour E. Harris, chairman of Harvard's Economics Department, thinks he has the 'answer to university financial woes.' He would let each student foot the entire cost of his education by having him pay the full $2,000 tuition cost instead of only $1,000 now prevailing. Dr. Harris believes the average family income in Ivy League universities runs from $12,000 to $20,000. If a parent earning $12,000 ($10,000 after taxes) had to pay $2,000 for his son's tuition, he would be paying 20 per cent of his total earnings. If, heaven forbid, the parent had a second son, he would be paying 40 per cent of his total earnings toward education alone. Such figures are prohibitive, and would be as confiscatory as taxes in eliminating worthy and desirable students. Dr. Harris does not have 'the answer.' He is merely shifting the burden from suffering universities to suffering parents." [32]

Economic considerations alone would dictate the elimination of non-endowed independent educational institutions. They are enterprises occupying noncompetitive positions in the academic world. But so is every other enterprise which is in competition with government-subsidized enterprises. If these institutions are to be eliminated because they cannot compete successfully with government schools in the market place of education, then we shall soon have complete government domination and control of the processes of education. Diversity in education will then be virtually non-existent. Conformity to state educational policy will then be the rule. If we are to preserve freedom in America, we may not allow government to become the sole educator of our youth. But how are we to keep our independent colleges and universities in existence to perform their essential function in a free democracy?

There are many reasons why foundations, corporations, private individuals, and various agencies of the Federal Government give grants running into many hundreds of millions of dollars yearly to a relatively small number of colleges and universities. But, with few exceptions, they demand that the institutions have a high-quality faculty, excellent research facilities, and research leisure. These are precisely the prerequisites that disqualify most independent institutions of higher learning. This means, in effect, that the more funds institutions have, the more they will receive; the less funds they have, the less they will receive. The consequent imbalance between the rapidly growing government and the selected independent institutions, on the one hand, and the large majority of independent institutions, on the other hand, is becoming more and more apparent. The facts are such that the immediate problem for many colleges and some universities is not one of development and growth but one of survival. Since present tuition pays only about one-half of educational costs, the general denial of other substantial sources of income threatens annihilation.

The foregoing analysis makes one thing perfectly clear—if governments, foundations, corporations, and private individuals continue their present policy of subsidizing higher education, there is little hope in the future for many independent universities and for many hundreds of independent colleges. The policy of grant-making adopted by the Federal Government and by foundations, and the prevailing policy of gift-giving adopted by corporations and individuals, aim to give further assistance to educational institutions that are already, with few exceptions and comparatively speaking, well financed. Such institutions have been getting more than the lion's share of grants and gifts. With these grants and gifts these colleges and universities have been able to improve and develop their educational activities. This is all to the good. But the problem of survival, to say nothing of improvement and development, of the nonprestige university and typical college remains. If these institutions are to judge from their past experience, they cannot plan the future in the expectation of receiving government and foundation grants or substantial corporation and individual gifts. They must urge upon government a new policy—a policy that will enable all educational institutions to improve and develop and thus to perform their essential function in our democracy.

Before analyzing the impact on independent educational institutions of the proposed government subsidization of the education of the individual student, it may be of advantage to discuss the nature of foundation grants, corporation and personal gifts to colleges and universities. What is the nature of such grants and gifts? Do they not have a public coloration about them because of their origin? If so, are they not "owed" proportionately to all educational institutions that serve a public purpose? The origin of such funds legitimately raises the question of their nature.

President John J. Theobald of Queens College of the City of New York declares that "private institutions in this country are in large measure supported by public funds. . . ." He emphasizes that he is not speaking about tax exemption but about "the fact that under our peculiar type of income tax set-up, the money our private colleges get in endowments is money that would otherwise go in large measure to the federal government in taxation, so that this is a way of tapping public support for higher education even in the private institutions. I don't see the great difference between that and putting it on the tax bills. I think in philosophy it is the same. . . ." [33] What is true of endowment gifts is, to a lesser degree, true of corporation and personal gifts for current and capital expenditures. If, for example, a single person has a taxed income for $150,000, a gift of $1,000 to an educational institution would cost him only $100. That is to say, every such $1,000 gift includes $900 that would go to the Federal Government if the gift were not made.

Personal gifts to colleges and universities are now deductible to the extent of 30 per cent of taxable net income and they are not subject to the gift tax regardless of their amount. Similar concessions are made to business corporations up to 5 per cent of their net income.

If President Theobald's argument is valid—and there seems to be no reason to reject it—then we must conclude that those independent colleges and universities that are highly endowed and the recipients of large foundation, corporation, and personal gifts are in effect supported in great measure by public funds. We must conclude, furthermore, that the only educational institutions that are not publicly supported, at least in the broad sense, are those "orphan" colleges and universities that are neither directly subsidized by government nor indirectly subsidized by government by means of tax concessions to foundations, corporations, and individuals.

This inequity does not necessarily follow upon the provisions of tax laws; it is consequent upon policies and practices adopted by foundations, corporations, and individuals. It remains to be demonstrated that such policies and practices can, in view of the origin of the funds contributed by such organizations and individuals, be rectified. It would seem that in view of the fact that a high proportion of such funds would go into government coffers but for tax provisions intended to make giving to *education* easy, such organizations and individuals who take advantage of these provisions have an obligation to make grants and gifts to educational institutions generally—so that the public purpose intended by the lawmaker will be best achieved. But since this reasoning is rejected by foundations, corporations, and individual philanthropists, the large majority of independent educational institutions must look elsewhere for the means of survival and development.

What we need is a Federal or state or Federal-state policy that will enable our 1,225 independent schools not only to survive but to develop and expand on the basis of solid academic standards. In this way alone can we hope to take care of the educational needs of American youth in the years ahead in a manner both economic and democratic. It is not economical to build scores of new colleges and universities to educate our youth at a cost of many billions of dollars, when the same objectives can in large measure be achieved by making it possible for existing and operating institutions to develop and expand to accommodate a large proportion of the student increase. Many of these schools could, at relatively little expenditure of money, double or quadruple their enrollment; others could, because of favorable location, increase their registration even more.

The certificate plan or the tax credit plan would enable American society to solve a great many of its educational problems, both economically and democratically. As pointed out in chapters above, it would not only be cheaper for the taxpayer but it would also ensure freedom of choice in education. Here we wish to consider what would be the effect of the direct subsidy method on independent schools and upon the whole educational picture in America.

Since tuition at independent schools pays only about half of the cost of education, these institutions are yearly faced with the all-but insurmountable problem of making up operational deficits that frequently run into many hundreds of thousands of dollars, and not infrequently to a million and more. Under such circumstances independent schools are not only reluctant to increase their enrollment, but a large proportion of them find it impossible to improve facilities and to pay salaries that are commensurate with state and endowed schools and with industry.

Many independent educators fear that raising tuition to something like the cost of education would effectively price them out of the education business. This would in effect bring about state monopoly in education. With tuition relatively low, from 50 to 80 per cent of the students in many colleges and universities must, nevertheless, work part-time to finance their education. Many other students are on partial or full scholarships. Raising tuition substantially would make it impossible for a large proportion of these students to attend an independent educational institution.

The proposed subsidization of students who attend independent colleges and universities would enable such institutions to charge tuition that more closely approximates the cost of education. A government subsidy of $500 would enable the typical independent school to charge a yearly tuition of from $700 to $1,000. The student or his parents would pay the difference between the subsidy and the actual tuition.

In many independent schools a tuition of from $700 to $1,000 approaches the cost of education. This would enable these institutions to turn their energies from a constant fight for survival to a program of development and improvement.

In view of the wide diversity of the educational problems that face our nation, it may be well to consider in greater detail some of the beneficial results that would in all probability flow from the adoption of the certificate or tax credit plan:

1. Many of the nation's small colleges would be able to double their enrollment without undertaking the expenditure of considerable sums of money. This would be a good thing. "Most small colleges have some classes that are too small to be either interesting or efficient," writes Dean Martin Quanbeck of Augsburg College. Dean Quanbeck, moreover, makes an important observation when he says that "in any college of fewer than 500 students, the number of classes with fewer than ten students is likely to be quite large. If this is not the case, the curricular offering is probably restricted to the point where student needs are not met adequately." [34] There are

about 800 such small institutions of higher education in our country. Dean Quanbeck estimates that his college, which numbers a little more than 500 students, could double its enrollment with a 50 or 60 per cent increase in faculty and administrative staff.[35]

In spite of the available facilities, the enrollment of the small colleges of the nation has not been increasing rapidly. Dean Quanbeck writes that enrollment statistics indicate two things:

(1) The larger colleges will no doubt experience the greatest pressures. (2) State institutions will be besieged by greater numbers of students than private ones. These trends are natural and not surprising. They can be explained largely in terms of differences in quality, prestige, and tuition costs. But the fact remains that those institutions which from the point of view of class size, at least, could best afford to take additional students probably will not get many. Those institutions which need to grow to operate more economically and efficiently may not see much growth. To put it in another way, those colleges in which additional students would really improve the quality of instruction are likely to get relatively small increases unless the larger colleges bar their doors or the smaller colleges are made more attractive in terms of quality and price of the program they offer.[36]

Dean Simeon E. Leland of Northwestern University makes the same point when he says that "many institutions could accommodate greatly increased numbers with no physical additions to plant and with relatively inexpensive expansions of staff, provided the added students were willing to go where the unfilled capacities exist." [37]

2. Independent institutions could use alumni contributions and individual and corporation gifts—to the extent that such are received by improved institutions—for purposes of expansion rather than for meeting operational deficits. With operational deficits virtually eliminated, many schools would be

in the position to increase their student capacity considerably on the basis of nontuition income. This would enable independent institutions to redress the balance between public and independent education. A decided imbalance is rapidly developing. Such a development definitely tends to circumscribe that freedom of mind and spirit that is essential for the preservation of democracy. In referring to the increasing percentage of colleges education "in public hands," public educator Theobald remarked: "This I think is something that we ought to think seriously about now, and take those steps necessary to temper it and maintain a balance." [38] He points out that during the past fifty years "enrollment in the private colleges has multiplied seven times, and during this same period, enrollment in the public colleges has multiplied 17 times." [39]

Dean Leland of Northwestern University also emphasizes the necessity of independent school expansion. He declared that "private institutions hate to face the fact that they must secure added funds to participate in the responsibilities which even the most conservative statistics indicate will inevitably devolve upon them." He observed that "unless private institutions meet this challenge and continue to take their fair proport'on of students they may as well give up their present position of influence in higher education." [40]

Of the total of $533,127,907 expended in 1953–1954 on increasing the physical properties of the 1,871 institutions of higher education, public institutions utilized 62.80 per cent and those under independent control 37.20 per cent. [41] The certificate or tax credit plan, since it would make possible the use of nontuition income for expansion and development, would enable the unendowed independent schools to increase their enrollment substantially. As a general rule, the endowed institutions are much larger in student enrollment than those with no endowment. In 1953–1954 the actual average for all endowed institutions was 1,561 students; that for unendowed institutions 689 students.[42]

3. Independent institutions could increase their classroom and laboratory facilities; they could acquire research equipment and the space to conduct research projects. Under present conditions of deficit operations, nontuition income is of necessity used all too exclusively to make up the difference between tuition income and educational costs. This makes it virtually impossible for these schools to acquire the new, expensive research equipment that is essential for up-to-date experimentation and research.

In the past the relatively small college has generally been the most productive of scientists. A recent study of the origins of American scientists revealed "the predominance of small institutions." [43] It was found that of the fifty most productive institutions for the years 1924–1934 only five graduated annually during this period more than two hundred students. After taking into consideration all significant variables, the study concludes that "there is reflected here a genuine difference in productivity related to the size of the institution." [44] The academic deterioration of these schools because of lack of income would be a great loss to scientific advancement and to Western civilization.

This deterioration, already begun, is definitely indicated by the inability of relatively small educational institutions to hire the needed Ph.D. physicists. The American Institute of Physics reported, after a survey of 490 college and university physics departments, that in these colleges a total of 688 Ph.D physicists would be needed at normal load to fill the existing vacancies. Half of the vacancies are in departments of six or less staff members.[45] The report says that "many of these institutions find it particularly difficult to attract physicists because of relatively low salary scales and because of the lack of research opportunities. Hence, it is doubtful whether the shortage of physics teachers in these small institutions can be corrected under prevailing conditions." [46] The American Institute of Physics alerts the reader to the consequences of this deterioration of the relatively small departments of physics. "Yet," the Institute makes clear, "half of the bachelor's degrees in physics in 1956–57 were granted by these colleges. There is in this situation," it warns, "a danger that the quality of instruction given not only to future physicists, but also to other undergraduate students of physics, is being seriously undermined." [47]

Improved research facilities would induce faculty members to remain at many independent colleges and universities who would otherwise go to institutions or laboratories where the means of research were assured.

4. Independent institutions could improve library facilities and secure the shelf holdings necessary to meet every academic requirement and to give students a wide and diversified range of books and periodicals.

5. These colleges and universities could increase faculty salaries very substantially, thus bringing them more into line with salaries paid in endowed and tax-supported institutions and in industries. Salary increases of from 60 to 80 per cent would enable independent institutions to engage competent faculty members and to hold them against attractive offers from industry, state institutions, and highly endowed colleges and universities.

If these institutions do not have the funds to hire and retain competent teachers, the quality of education will of necessity deteriorate. Referring to today's salary scale in all too many educational institutions, Mr. Devereaux Josephs, chairman of the President's Committee on Education Beyond the High School, remarked that "you can always find someone who is willing to teach at current salaries. Unfortunately, it is not enough to get 'someone.' We need the best possible teachers, and we should be ready to pay for them." [48]

6. Better teaching conditions and better salaries would induce many qualified young men and women who now go into industrial work to enter the teaching profession. In 1955 and 1956 about three out of four doctor's degree graduates in the sciences entered noneducational occupations.[49] A decisive factor is a salary differential that is roughly from $1,000 to $3,000 higher in industry. The Research Division of the National Education Association reports that "the colleges and universities are fighting a losing battle as they seek to obtain the services of the most coveted groups of graduates at the doctorate level." [50] This flight of potential scholars from the classroom and laboratory will, in the long run, have disastrous consequences for higher education, research, scientific development, and for industry itself. It is the sure road to universal mediocrity. The scientist is born, under proper conditions, on the school campus; he is not born in the industrial laboratory.

Better morale among the teaching faculty is the best inducement to get young men and women to enter the teaching profession. A better faculty morale in the 1,225 independent colleges and universities would undoubtedly bring many thousands of qualified individuals into the teaching ranks. The teaching profession, like other professions, must be its own best reason why the young seek admission to its ranks. If the teaching profession is going to be successful in recruiting the best minds, teaching itself must be viewed by the public as a profession of prestige. The public mind today all too readily discounts the prestige value of a profession whose members have a salary income considerably less than the local bricklayer and carpenter.

If all independent colleges and universities could pay salaries commensurate with the dignity of the teaching profession, the prestige of the profession in the public mind would rapidly rise. And with the rising of prestige, qualified young men and women would be ambitious to enter the lecture hall and the research laboratory.

7. Independent universities would have the budgetary resources to give a large number of substantial graduate assistantships and fellowships. Thus students who complete their undergraduate studies with a good scholastic record in one or other of the small colleges would experience little difficulty continuing their education on the graduate level. Assistant or fellowship experience would lead many of these students to continue the academic life beyond graduation.

The increased income from higher tuition would enable many universities to strengthen their graduate programs. This would in turn bring about a decentralization of the important work of training future college teachers, a work that is now too highly centralized in a very small number of graduate schools for the good of the teaching profession.

8. Independent colleges and universities, with an income of $500 from each student assured, could have a liberal scholarship program for needy students. This would make it possible for qualified but needy students living near one or the other of the 1,225 independent institutions to pursue their education with little or no cost to them. Furthermore, such a liberal scholarship program would make it possible for many excellent students who must now work part-time off campus to pay their tuition to give full time to the pursuit of learning. This would be to the advantage of both the student and American society.

9. Every community with a high-quality independent college or university would take even greater pride in its institution of higher learning than it now does. The well qualified faculty of such institutions would lend prestige to the community. Parents would not hesitate to send their children to

such schools, knowing that they have adequate facilities and competent faculties.

The president of such a college or university would seek contributions from individuals and industrial corporations for an institution that is in every sense one of the greatest assets of the community; he would no longer go about like a beggar seeking funds to calk up the holes of a ship constantly in danger of sinking.

\* \* \*

This book may well be concluded with a summary of some of the considerations that argue forcefully in favor of direct government subsidies to independent-school children and college students to enable them to pay in part a tuition approximating the cost of education in the school of their choice. These are (1) the avoidance of constitutional issues; (2) the inauguration of a policy of freedom of choice in education, thus ensuring substantial equality and freedom of mind and freedom of religion in schooling; (3) a means of implementing society's educational obligations to independent-school children and students; (4) new opportunities and greater challenges for gifted children and students; (5) the moderation of the trend toward the complete socialization of education on every level; (6) the preservation of voluntary associations in the field of education which, together with other such associations, form a bulwark for the defense of freedom; (7) substantial savings for the taxpayer; (8) the maintenance of competition, diversity, and free enterprise in education; (9) increased educational opportunities for the qualified but needy young man or woman; (10) the re-establishment and retention of some balance between independent and government education; (11) higher quality teaching on every level of education; (12) the entrance of an increasing number of competent individuals into the teaching profession; and (13) greater ability of educational institutions to accommodate the increasing influx of children and students in a manner that is economic and best calculated to effect the intellectual development of our nation's children and students in a way consistent with the constitutional guarantee of freedom of mind and freedom of religion.

# Notes

## Chapter I (pages 1–22)

1. Ernest Barker, *Principles of Social and Political Theory* (Oxford: The Clarendon Press, 1951), p. 268.
2. *Ibid.*, p. 274.
3. It must be recognized that voluntary groups are not all beyond violating the freedom of their members, e.g., the Teamsters union.
4. Barker, *op. cit.*, p. 274.
5. *Ibid.*, p. 276.
6. R. M. MacIver, *The Web of Government* (New York: The Macmillan Company, 1949), p. 109.
7. *Ibid.*
8. *Ibid.*, p. 411.
9. *Ibid.*
10. Alfred North Whitehead, *Adventures of Ideas* (New York: The Macmillan Company, 1933), p. 73.
11. *Ibid.*
12. *Ibid.*, p. 69.
13. *Ibid.*, p. 73.
14. *Ibid.*, pp. 73–74.
15. Joseph Lecler, S.J., *The Two Sovereignties* (New York: Philosophical Library, 1952), *passim.*
16. Whitehead, *op. cit.*, p. 75.
17. Barker, *Reflections on Government* (London: Oxford University Press, 1942), p. 11.
18. *Ibid.*, pp. 15–16.
19. MacIver, *op. cit.*, p. 429.
20. John Stuart Mill, *On Liberty* . . . (New York: The Macmillan Company, 1926), p. 137.
21. Barker, *Reflections on Government*, p. 26.
22. MacIver, *op. cit.*, p. 441.
23. Barker, *Reflections on Government*, p. 28.
24. *Ibid.*
25. Whitehead, *op. cit.*, p. 64.
26. Mill, *op. cit.*, p. 126.

27. These points will be elaborated in a later chapter.

28. Barker, *Principles of Social and Political Theory*, p. 277.

29. *The Report of the Commission on Financing Higher Education: Nature and Needs of Higher Education* (New York: Columbia University Press, 1952), p. 31.

30. See, for example, Milton Friedman, "The Role of Government in Education," in *Economics and the Public Interest*, edited by Robert A. Solo (New Brunswick: Rutgers University Press, 1955), *passim*.

31. Friedman, *op. cit.*; Procter Thomson, "Educational News and Editorial Comment," *The School Review*, LXIII (April, 1955), 189–200.

32. Friedman, *op. cit.*, p. 127.

33. *Ibid.*, pp. 127–128.

34. Thomson, *op. cit.*, p. 190.

35. *Ibid.*

36. *College and University Bulletin* (Nov. 15 and Dec. 1, 1956), quoted in "What The Colleges Are Doing" (Winter, 1957), p. 3.

37. *Second Report to the President. The President's Committee on Education Beyond the High School* (July, 1957), p. 11.

38. From copy of resolutions adopted by the Association of American Colleges, Jan. 9, 1958, Miami, Florida.

39. *Higher Education and National Affairs*, issued by American Council on Education, VII (Jan. 28, 1958), p. 2. See also *Higher Education and National Affairs*, VII (June 13, 1958), pp. 3, 4–5, 8.

40. Thomson, *op. cit.*, pp. 190–191.

41. *New York Times*, June 9, 1958.

## Chapter II (*pages 23–37*)

1. Burton Confrey, *Secularism in American Education: Its History* (Washington: The Catholic University of America, 1931), pp. 124–125.

2. *Everson* v. *Board of Education*, 330 U.S. 1 (1947); *McCollum* v. *Board of Education*, 333 U.S. 203 (1948). To what extent the absolute-separation doctrine enunciated in these cases has been modified in *Zorach* v. *Clauson*, 343 U.S. 306 (1952), is difficult to determine, although the Court was, manifestly, following the *McCollum* precedent.

3. Dr. Will Herberg declares that "when the public schools system first came into being in this country, it was nonsectarian rather

than non-religious. And nonsectarian in those days meant all-Protestant, since non-Protestant groups were of relatively little social or cultural importance in most parts of the nation. It was taken for granted that religion, in the generalized Protestant sense, was the foundation of education, though the schools were not of course to be used to favor one Protestant denomination over another." "The Sectarian Conflict Over Church and State," *Commentary*, 14 (Nov., 1952), 450–451.

4. Gustavus Myers, *The History of Bigotry in the United States* (New York: Random House, 1943), *passim*; Ray Allen Billington, *The Protestant Crusade* (New York: The Macmillan Company, 1938), *passim*. For background see: Sister Mary Augustina (Ray), *American Opinion of Roman Catholicism in the Eighteenth Century* (New York: Columbia University Press, 1936).

5. Robert Fairchild Cushman, "Public Support of Religious Education in American Constitutional Law," *Illinois Law Review*, XLV (1950), 335.

6. Bernard Iddings Bell, "Know How vs. Know Why," *Life*, Oct. 16, 1950, p. 98.

7. Sherman M. Smith, *The Relation of the State to Religious Education in Massachusetts* (Syracuse, N.Y.: Syracuse University Book Store, 1926), p. 211, italics added.

8. *Dunn* v. *Chicago Industrial School for Girls*, 280 Ill. 613, 618 (1917). See *Dunn* v. *The Addison Manual Training School for Boys*, 281 Ill. 352 (1917), *Trost* v. *Ketteler Training School*, 282 Ill. 504 (1918), *St. Hedwig's School* v. *Cook County*, 289 Ill. 432 (1919), *Craig* v. *Mercy Hospital—Street Memorial*, 45 So. 2d 809 (1950), *Murrow Indian Orphans Home* v. *Childers*, 197 Okla. 249 (1946). In this case which involved a Baptist orphanage, the Supreme Court of Oklahoma reiterated the value-received doctrine. It declared (p. 251) that so long as the contracts between the state and denominational institutions "involve the element of substantial return to the state and do not amount to a gift, donation or appropriation to the institution having no relevance to the affairs of the state, there is no constitutional provision offended." The contracts with the Baptist orphanage were held constitutional. *Schade* v. *Allegheny County Institution Dist.*, 126 A.2d 911 (1956). The issue in this case was whether the use of tax monies for the support, care and maintenance of neglected and dependent children in Baptist and Catholic orphanages violates the state constitution and the First Amendment "no establishment" clause made applicable to the states by way of the due process clause of the Fourteenth Amendment. The Supreme Court of Pennsylvania de-

clared that "the plaintiffs have failed to prove any appropriations have, and are being made by [the Institution District] for charitable, educational or benevolent purposes to any denominational or sectarian institutions, or that any public funds are administered through such forbidden channels, or put under their control as an aid to such institutions. . . . All the plaintiffs proved was that the monies received by the defendant institutions were in partial reimbursement for the cost of room and board of such minors." The court said, further, that the use of public monies for the care of orphans in denominational institutions does not violate the "no establishment" clause. It asserted that "the appellant argues that . . . payments to the denominational . . . defendants tend toward governmental 'establishment of religion' and, consequently, are violative of the Fourteenth Amendment. It is unnecessary to devote much time to this contention. The Supreme Court [of the United States] has, in principle, settled it adversely to the appellant's position. See *Everson* v. *Board of Education*, 330 U.S. 1 (1947), where it was held that a State's use of public tax funds for the transportation of pupils to and from sectarian schools did not serve to promote the establishment of religion."

9. *Ibid.*, p. 619.

10. *Higher Education and National Affairs*, issued by American Council on Education, VII (Jan. 28, 1958), p. 2.

11. *Second Report to the President. The President's Committee on Education Beyond the High School* (Washington: U.S. Government Printing Office, 1957), p. 96, italics added.

12. *Cochran* v. *Board of Education*, 281 U.S. 370, 375 (1930).

13. *Everson* v. *Board of Education*, 330 U.S. 1, 16 (1947).

14. "An Act for establishing Religious Freedom, January 16, 1786," *Documents of American History*, ed. by Henry Steele Commager (New York: Appleton-Century-Crofts & Co., 1949), pp. 125–126.

15. *Annual Report of the United States Department of Health, Education, and Welfare* (1955), pp. 76, 77.

16. *Ibid.*

17. *Second Report to the President. The President's Committee on Education Beyond the High School* (Washington: U.S. Government Printing Office, 1957), pp. 51–52.

## *Chapter III (pages 38–61)*

1. Henry P. Van Dusen, *God in Education* (New York: Charles Scribner's Sons, 1951), p. 83.

2. Sir Walter Moberly, *The Crisis in the University* (London: SCM Press Ltd., 1949), pp. 55–56, 27.

3. *Pierce v. Society of Sisters*, 268 U.S. 510 (1925).

4. *Ibid.*, p. 535.

5. *Frost v. Railroad Commission*, 271 U.S. 583, 594 (1926).

6. *Ibid.*

7. *Ibid.*

8. *American Communications Assn. v. Douds*, 339 U.S. 382, 417 (1950), concurring opinion.

9. Willcox, 41 *Cornell Law Quarterly*, 12, 43–44 (1955).

10. The problem of securing the educational rights of children, regardless of religious belief, has not been completely solved in some other Western democracies. However, no country which subscribes to the principles of freedom has so adamantly refused to face up to the problem as has the United States.

11. See *Grosjean v. American Press Co.*, 297 U.S. 233 (1936), *Jones v. Opelika*, 319 U.S. 103 (1943); *Murdock v. Pennsylvania*, 319 U.S. 105 (1943).

12. Willcox, *op. cit.*, p. 45.

13. *Ibid.*

14. *Prince v. Massachusetts*, 321 U.S. 158, 166 (1944).

15. *Everson v. Board of Education*, 330 U.S. 1, 18 (1947).

16. *Pierce v. Society of Sisters*, 268 U.S. 510 (1925).

17. *Ibid.*, pp. 534–535.

18. *Meyer v. Nebraska*, 262 U.S. 390 (1923).

19. *Ibid.*, p. 410.

20. Willcox, *op. cit.*, p. 56.

21. *Ibid.*, p. 44.

22. Wilber G. Katz, "The Freedom to Believe," *Atlantic*, 192 (Oct., 1953), 66.

23. *Ibid.*, pp. 68–69.

24. *West Virginia State Board of Education v. Barnette*, 319 U.S. 624, 637 (1943).

25. Bernard Iddings Bell, *Crisis in Education* (New York: McGraw-Hill Book Company, 1949), p. 222.

26. *Ibid.*

27. *American Communications Assn. v. Douds*, 339 U.S. 382, 446 (1950), dissenting opinion.

28. Bell, *op. cit.*, p. 222.

29. *Ibid.*
30. *American Communications Assn.* v. *Douds*, 339 U.S. 382, 421 (1950), concurring opinion.
31. Mr. Justice Douglas, "The Black Silence of Fear," *The New York Times Magazine*, Jan. 13, 1952.
32. *Ibid.*
33. *West Virginia Board of Education* v. *Barnette*, 319 U.S. 624, 641–642 (1943).
34. *Ibid.*
35. William Ebenstein, *Great Political Thinkers* (New York: Rinehart & Company, 1956, 2nd ed.), p. 511.
36. *Ibid.*, p. 509.
37. *Ibid.*
38. *Ibid.*
39. Bell, *op. cit.*, pp. 189–190.
40. *Ibid.*
41. *Ibid.*, p. 191.
42. *Ibid.*
43. Mill, *op. cit.*, p. 126.
44. *Ibid.*, p. 135.
45. *Ibid.*, p. 126.
46. *West Virginia Board of Education* v. *Barnette*, 319 U.S. 624, 642 (1943).
47. *Chance* v. *Mississippi State Textbook Rating and Purchasing Board*, 200 So. 706, 710 (1941).
48. *American Communications Assn.* v. *Douds*, 339 U.S. 382, 442 (1948), concurring and dissenting, each in part.
49. *Ibid.*
50. *Ibid.*, p. 443.
51. *Ibid.*
52. *Ibid.*, p. 439.
53. *Minersville School Dist.* v. *Gobitis*, 310 U.S. 586 (1940).
54. *Ibid.*, p. 602.
55. *Ibid.*, p. 604.
56. *Ibid.*
57. Van Dusen, *op. cit.*, p. 83.
58. *Minersville School Dist.* v. *Gobitis*, 310 U.S. 586, 604 (1940), Mr. Justice Stone, dissenting opinion.

59. *Ibid.*, p. 606. Mr. Justice Stone, dissenting opinion.
60. *Ibid.*, pp. 606–607, dissenting opinion.
61. *Dennis* v. *U.S.* 341 U.S. 494, 556 (1951), concurring opinion.
62. Ebenstein, *op. cit.*, p. 504.
63. *Ibid.*
64. *Ibid.*
65. *Ibid.*
66. *West Virginia Board of Education* v. *Barnette,* 319 U.S. 624, 641 (1943).
67. *Minersville School Dist.* v. *Gobitis,* 310 U.S. 586, 606–607 (1940), dissenting opinion, italics added.
68. *New York Times,* June 23, 1958.
69. *Ibid.*

## Chapter IV (pages 62–77)

1. M. M. Boring, "Will Scholarships Give U.S. Better-Trained Scientists," *U.S. News & World Report,* Jan. 24, 1958, p. 78.
2. Bernard Iddings Bell, "Know How vs. Know Why," *Life,* Oct. 16, 1950, p. 98.
3. Arnold O. Beckman, Address before the Los Angeles Chamber of Commerce, June 22, 1956.
4. *Time,* Dec. 24, 1956. Since government schools constitute a virtual monopoly on the elementary and secondary levels of education, they have been the object of serious criticism by those who decry the quality of elementary and secondary education. It cannot, obviously, be deduced from this that some, at least, or many of our independent schools are not deserving of the same criticism.
5. Beckman, *op. cit.*
6. Arthur Bestor, "What Went Wrong With U.S. Schools," *U.S. News & World Report,* Jan. 24, 1958, p. 69.
7. *Ibid.*, p. 70. It is not undemocratic to recognize the fact that students are endowed with varying degrees of intellectual ability. And if we recognize the fact, then we must, in justice to the individual gifted students and to American society, provide such students with a program of studies that will challenge them to the full extent of their ability. The Rockefeller Brothers Fund report on "The Pursuit of Excellence: Education and the Future of America" recommends for students of considerable academic ability: "In addition to the general education prescribed for all—four years of English, three to four years of social studies, one year of mathematics and one year

of science—the academically talented student should have two to three additional years of science, three additional years of mathematics, and at least three years of a foreign language. For certain students the study of a second foreign language, for at least three years, might replace the fourth year of mathematics and the third year of science. Particularly with respect to the highest-priority subjects, we must modernize and improve the quality of the courses themselves." Referring to the quantity and quality of our science education, the report declares that "the crisis in our science education is not an invention of the newspapers, or scientists, or the Pentagon. It is a real crisis." *New York Times*, June 23, 1958.

8. Msgr. Thomas J. Quigley, *Catholic Herald-Citizen*, May 12, 1956.

9. *Ibid.*

10. *Ibid.*

11. Bestor, *op. cit.*, p. 70.

12. *Ibid.*, p. 71. This raises the question of the proper objectives of our schools. The Rockefeller Brothers Fund report, which demands high-level performance of our gifted students, raises the same question when it says that "our schools will need . . . an unsparing re-examination of current practices, patterns of organization and objectives." *New York Times*, June 23, 1958.

13. President Dwight D. Eisenhower, "Science in the National Security," *New York Times*, Nov. 14, 1957. After returning from a month-long study of education in the USSR, Dr. Lawrence G. Derthick, Commissioner of Education, one of ten American educators who made the study, declared, June 13, 1958, to the National Press Club: "What we have seen has amazed us in one outstanding particular: We are simply not prepared for the degree to which the U.S.S.R., as a nation, is committed to education as a means of national advancement. Everywhere we went we saw indication after indication of what we could only conclude amounted to a total commitment to education.

"Our major reaction therefore is one of astonishment—and I choose the word carefully—at the extent to which this seems to have been accomplished. For what it is worth, ten American educators came away sobered by what they saw. . . . The importance of science in Soviet education is a matter which is unquestioned. Biology, chemistry, physics and astronomy are required of every pupil regardless of his individual interest or aspirations. . . . At every turn in our travels we were struck by the emphasis and attention paid to the study of languages in the schools. . . . It may also be of interest to know that approximately 46 per cent of the ten-year school pupils are studying English, 6 per cent German and

20 per cent French. We were also informed by the Minister of Education that efforts are being made to increase the emphasis on conversational competence.

"Everywhere in Russia there were evidences not only of passionate love of country but a burning desire to surpass the United States in education, in production, in standard of living, in world trade—and in athletics. . . . In education the spirit is a race for knowledge, for supremacy in a way of life and in world leadership. The Russian attitude is, as one Soviet official told us, 'We believe in a planned society, you in individual initiative. Let time tell.' They are convinced that time is on their side and they can win world supremacy through education and hard work.

"This conviction is basic to all of their efforts and all of their plans for the future. Education is paramount. It is a kind of grand passion—this conviction that children, schools and hard work will win them their place in the sun, and on the moon." *New York Times,* June 14, 1958.

14. Bestor, *op. cit.,* p. 71.
15. *Time,* Feb. 17, 1958.
16. *Ibid.*
17. *Ibid.*
18. *World-Herald,* Omaha, June 24, 1956.
19. *New York Times,* Dec. 19, 1956.
20. Jan. 2, 1958, reprinted in the *Congressional Record,* Jan. 15, 1958.
21. *New York Times,* Nov. 21, 1956.
22. *Ibid.*
23. *New York Times,* July 20, 1956.
24. *Ibid.,* April 5, 1956.
25. *Ibid.,* May 21, 1956, reprinted in the *Congressional Record,* July 28, 1956, Appendix, p. A5981.
26. *Ibid.*
27. *Ibid.*
28. John A. Hannah, Address delivered to the Michigan Schoolmasters' Club, Ann Arbor, May 11, 1956.
29. Seymour St. John, "The Fifth Freedom," *Saturday Review,* XXXVI, Oct. 10, 1953, p. 24.
30. *Ibid.*
31. Felix Schelling, quoted by Dr. John A. Hannah in Address delivered to the Michigan Schoolmasters' Club, Ann Arbor, May 11, 1956.

32. *Ibid.*

33. *New York Times*, June 23, 1958.

## Chapter V *(pages 78–110)*

1. *Documents of American History*, ed. by Henry Steele Commager, p. 131, italics added.

2. *Ibid.*, p. 100.

3. *Ibid.*, p. 173, italics added.

4. *Ibid.*

5. Seymour St. John, "The Fifth Freedom," *Saturday Review*, XXXVI (Oct. 10, 1953), p. 24, italics added. Regarding teacher-education, Dr. Will Herberg declares that "the most influential educational philosophies and centers of teachers' training are self-consciously secularist, and so is educational practice in almost every part of the country."—"The Sectarian Conflict Over Church and State," *Commentary*, 14 (Nov. 1952), 451.

6. James J. Walsh, *Education of the Founding Fathers of the Republic* (New York: Fordham University Press, 1935), p. 85.

7. *Ibid.*, pp. 86–87.

8. *Ibid.*, p. 111.

9. *Ibid.*, pp. 117–118.

10. *Ibid.*, pp. 118–119.

11. *Ibid.*, pp. 119–120. The report of the Board of Overseers of Harvard University in 1869 stated: "We should all labor together to make Harvard a noble University,—a seat of learning which should attract the best teachers and most ardent students,—a University which shall retain all the good of the past, and go forward to welcome the advancing light of the future. So may the priceless gift of our fathers be transmitted to our children, not only unimpaired, but constantly renewed and bettered. Let each generation do its part to make it more worthy of this great country, this advancing civilization, this ripening age. In the largest sense, let it be devoted to Christ, the great teacher of truth, and to his Church, the great means of human education." Quoted from Samuel Eliot Morison, *Freedom in Contemporary Society* (Boston: Little, Brown and Company, 1956), p. 144.

12. *Documents of American History*, p. 100.

13. Benjamin Wright, *American Interpretations of Natural Law* (Cambridge: Harvard University Press, 1931), p. 88, note 105.

14. *Ibid.*

15. *Ibid.*, pp. 90–91.
16. James Otis, *The Rights of the British Colonies Asserted and Proved* (1764), p. 47.
17. Dwight D. Eisenhower, *New York Times*, Feb. 21, 1955.
18. *Zorach* v. *Clauson*, 343 U.S. 306, 313 (1952).
19. Thomas F. Woodlock, *Wall Street Journal*, Aug. 27, 1945, reprinted July 2, 1954.
20. Thomas Jefferson, *Notes on the State of Virginia*, ed. by William Peden (Chapel Hill: The University of North Carolina Press, 1955), p. 163.
21. Saul K. Padover, ed., *The Complete Jefferson* (New York: Duell, Sloane & Pierce, 1943), pp. 957–958.
22. Francis M. Rogers, *St. Louis Review*, Feb. 14, 1958. See chapter 10, p. 157. Nathan M. Pusey, president of Harvard University, in his baccalaureate address, June 8, 1958, taking a critical look at the academic "way of life which . . . proceeds deliberately without concern for religion," sharply raised the question of censorship by selection in educational institutions when he declared that the university has a duty to help students "ask the right questions—and *all* the questions." *Time*, June 23, 1958, and *New York Times*, June 9, 1958, italics added.
23. Charles Malik, *St. Louis Register*, June 11, 1954.
24. *Ibid.*
25. *Ibid.*
26. W. G. Peck, *The Salvation of Modern Man*, p. 83. Quoted in E. L. Mascall, B.D., *He Who Is: A Study in Traditional Theism* (London: Longmans, Green & Co., 1943), p. 3.
27. Sir Walter Moberly, *The Crisis in the University*, p. 68.
28. Robert Bernerd Anderson, Address delivered at Baylor University Conference on American Ideals, Oct. 17, 1953. Printed copy.
29. *Ibid.*
30. *Ibid.*
31. *Ibid.*
32. *Ibid.*
33. *Ibid.*
34. Henry P. Van Dusen, *God in Education*, p. 53.
35. *Ibid.*, p. 54.
36. *Ibid.*, p. 54.
37. Bernard Iddings Bell, "Know How vs. Know Why," *Life*, Oct. 16, 1950, p. 97.

38. *Ibid.*

39. Van Dusen, *op. cit.*, p. 66, italics added.

40. *Ibid.*, p. 71.

41. *Ibid.*, p. 80.

42. Edward B. Pusey, *Collegiate and Professional Teaching and Discipline*, p. 25, in Moberly, *op. cit.*, p. 265.

43. Van Dusen, *op. cit.*, pp. 81–82, italics added.

44. Hastings Rashdall, *The Universities of Europe in the Middle Ages*, III (Oxford: Clarendon Press, 1936), 442.

45. Van Dusen, *op. cit.*, pp. 82–83, italics added.

46. *West Virginia State Board of Education* v. *Barnette*, 319 U.S. 624, 642 (1943).

47. Moberly, *op. cit.*, pp. 55–56, 27.

48. *Illinois ex. rel. McCollum* v. *Board of Education*, 333 U.S. 203 (1948).

49. Will Herberg, "The Sectarian Conflict over Church and State," *Commentary*, 14 (Nov., 1952), 451.

50. Bernard Iddings Bell, *Crisis in Education*, p. 222.

51. F. Ernest Johnson, *Catholic Universe Bulletin*, Cleveland, Feb. 3, 1950.

52. *Ibid.* President Nathan Pusey of Harvard declared in his baccalaureate address of 1958 that religion in a secular university confronts "the advance of secularization." So great have been the successes of secularism, he said, that it "has itself become a *faith* and raised a hope that man can through his own efforts—without God —solve all the remaining problems which stand between him and a secular paradise on earth." Secularism, maintains President Pusey, forms a new kind of fundamentalism whose "temples may be laboratories and factories, perhaps also libraries . . . Its noxious influence—noxious I believe to spirit, imagination and to mind— works among us almost unopposed." *Time*, June 23, 1958, italics added. Dr. Pusey is convinced that "secularization is today, as we all know, a very serious stumbling block in our society." Secularism or secularization is defined by President Pusey as an "attachment to a way of life in which there is neither need or place for religion." *New York Times*, June 9, 1958.

53. *Everson* v. *Board of Education*, 330 U.S. 1 (1947).

54. Johnson, *ibid.*

55. Edward McCrady, *Our Sunday Visitor*, Jan. 23, 1955.

56. *Ibid.*

57. *Ibid.*
58. *Ibid.*
59. *Ibid.*
60. *Ibid.*
61. *Ibid.*
62. *Ibid.*
63. See John L. Thomas, S.J., "Parental Responsibility Left at the School Door," *Homiletic and Pastoral Review,* LVIII (June, 1957), p. 815.
64. Bell, *Crisis in Education,* p. 138.
65. *Ibid.,* p. 139.
66. *Ibid.,* pp. 139–140.
67. *Ibid.,* p. 145.
68. *The Tablet,* May 31, 1958.
69. *Time,* June 23, 1958.
70. *The Tablet,* May 31, 1958.
71. Walter Donald Kring, *New York Times,* Feb. 3, 1958.
72. *Ibid.*
73. *The Tablet,* editorial, March 1, 1958.
74. *Ibid.*
75. *Kovacs* v. *Cooper,* 336 U.S. 77, 97 (1949), concurring opinion.
76. Alexis de Tocqueville, *France Before the Revolution of 1789,* in Henry Hazlitt, "The Road to Totalitarianism," in *On Freedom and Free Enterprise,* ed. by Mary Sennholz (Princeton, N.J.: D. Van Nostrand Co., Inc., 1956), pp. 82–83.

## Chapter VI *(pages 111–120)*

1. *Hayes* v. *Missouri,* 120 U.S. 68, 71 (1887).
2. *Barbier* v. *Connolly,* 113 U.S. 27, 32 (1885).
3. *McCabe* v. *Atchison, T. & S.F.R.R.,* 235 U.S. 151, 161 (1914).
4. *Frost* v. *Railroad Commission,* 271 U.S. 583, 594 (1926).
5. *Railway Express Agency* v. *New York,* 336 U.S. 106, 112 (1949), concurring opinion.
6. *Ibid.,* pp. 112–113.
7. George K. Gardner, "Liberty, The State, and the School," *Law and Contemporary Problems,* XX (Winter, 1955), p. 194.
8. *Truax* v. *Corrigan,* 257 U.S. 312, 333 (1921).

9. *Gulf, C. & S.F.R. Co. v. Ellis*, 165 U.S 150, 159 (1897).

10. For an able discussion of equal protection see Joseph Tussman and Jacobus ten Broek, "The Equal Protection of Laws," *California Law Review*, XXXVII (1944), 341 *passim*.

11. *Quaker City Cab Co. v. Pennsylvania*, 277 U.S. 389, 405 (1928).

12. *Royster Guano Co. v. Virginia*, 253 U.S. 412, 415 (1920).

13. *Truax v. Corrigan*, 257 U.S. 312, 337 (1921), italics added.

14. *Chance v. Mississippi State Textbook Rating and Purchasing Board*, 200 So. 706, 710 (1941), italics added.

15. *Ibid.*

16. *Ibid.*

### Chapter VII (pages 121–132)

1. *Meyer v. Nebraska*, 262 U.S. 390 (1923); *Pierce v. Society of Sisters*, 268 U.S. 510 (1925); *Prince v. Massachusetts*, 321 U.S. 158 (1944); *Everson v. Board of Education*, 330 U.S. 1 (1947).

2. Wilber G. Katz, "The Freedom to Believe," *Atlantic*, 192 (Oct., 1953), 69.

3. *Everson v. Board of Education*, 330 U.S. 1, 23–24 (1947), dissenting opinion. "Secularism has taken over in the United States," Paul Hutchinson writes in *The New Ordeal of Christianity*; in Eugene Carson Blake's judgment as expressed in his *Christian Faith: Bulwark of Freedom*: "we are living in a nation that is largely secular and in a secular age"; the impact of secularism, Frederick K. Wentz says in *The Times Test the Church*, "is now marked across the whole earth." Quoted in a book review in *Social Order*, June, 1957, by Edward Duff, S.J.

4. *Illinois ex rel. McCollum v. Board of Education*, 333 U.S. 203 (1948).

5. Raymond B. Culver, *Horace Mann and Religion in the Massachusetts Public Schools* (New Haven: Yale University Press, 1929), p. 235.

6. *Documents of American History*, ed. by Henry Steele Commager, p. 125.

7. *Ibid.*, p. 126.

8. *Jones v. Opelika*, 316 U.S. 584, 608 (1942), dissenting opinion.

9. *Murdock v. Pennsylvania*, 319 U.S. 105, 112 (1943).

10. *Ibid.*

11. *Documents of American History*, p. 125.

12. Henry P. Van Dusen, *God in Education*, p. 71.

13. Bernard Iddings Bell, *Crisis in Education*, p. 222.
14. Will Herberg, "The Sectarian Conflict Over Church and State," *Commentary*, 14 (Nov., 1952), p. 451.
15. Sir Walter Moberly, *The Crisis in the University*, p. 56.
16. Katz, *op. cit.*, p. 67.
17. *Ibid.*
18. *Everson* v. *Board of Education*, 333 U.S. 1, 18 (1947).
19. Katz, *op. cit.*, p. 68.
20. *Ibid.*
21. *Ibid.* Four states have adopted the principle and practice of freedom of choice in education in their college-scholarship programs. Winners of state-provided scholarships in New York, California, Maryland, and Illinois are not coerced to attend state-controlled colleges and universities as a condition of receiving the award; they have the freedom of choice which enables them to attend any recognized institution of higher education within the state. All other states with scholarship programs without exception, it seems, condition the receiving of such awards, as well as regular state-educational subsidies through "free" education, on the surrender of the constitutional right of freedom of choice in education.
22. *Ibid.*, pp. 68–69.
23. *Ibid.*, p. 69.
24. *Register*, Nov. 13, 1953.
25. Procter Thomson, "Educational News and Editorial Comment," *School Review: A Journal of Secondary Education*, LXIII (April, 1955), 195.
26. Bell, *op. cit.*, p. 222.
27. *New World*, April 27, 1951.
28. Herberg, *op. cit.*, p. 453.

## Chapter VIII (*pages 133–142*)

1. Bernard Iddings Bell, *Crisis in Education*, p. 145.
2. *New York Times*, June 3, 1958.
3. *Ibid.*
4. *Ibid.*
5. *New York Times*, June 5, 1958.
6. *Ibid.*
7. Will Herberg, "Justice for Religious Schools," *America*, XCVIII (Nov. 15, 1957), 191.

8. *Ibid.*
9. James J. Walsh, *Education of the Founding Fathers of the Republic, passim.*
10. *Ibid.*, p. 63, italics added.
11. *Ibid.*, pp. 96–97.
12. Quoted in Walsh, *op. cit.*, p. 84.
13. Quoted in *I. F. Stone's Weekly*, V (Nov. 18, 1957), 1.

### Chapter IX (*pages 143–150*)

1. Milton Friedman, "The Role of Government in Education," in *Economics and the Public Interest*, ed. by Robert A. Solo (New Brunswick, N.J.: Rutgers University Press, 1955), p. 129.
2. Procter Thomson, "Educational News and Editorial Comment," *School Review*, LXVIII (April, 1955), p. 192.
3. Friedman, *op. cit.*, p. 130.
4. Arthur Bestor, "We Are Less Educated than 50 Years Ago," *U.S. News & World Report*, XLI (Nov. 30, 1956), p. 74.

### Chapter X (*pages 151–163*)

1. Address given at Loomis School Dinner in Honor of Frank and Frances Gubbs, May 7, 1953.
2. *Ibid.*
3. *Ibid.*
4. Procter Thomson, "Educational News and Editorial Comment," *School Review*, LXIII (April, 1955), p. 191.
5. *Ibid.*
6. Hans F. Sennholz, "On Democracy," essay in *On Freedom and Free Enterprise*, ed. by Mary Sennholz, p. 65.
7. *Minersville School Dist.* v. *Gobitis*, 310 U.S. 586 (1940).
8. Sennholz, *op. cit.*, p. 65.
9. *Ibid.*, pp. 65–66.
10. W. Homer Turner, "Public Relations Beyond the Campus," booklet, p. 4.
11. *Ibid.*, p. 6.
12. F. Morstein Marx, "Administrative Ethics and the Rule of Law," *American Political Science Review*, XVIII (Dec., 1949), p. 1139.
13. Robert M. Hutchins, *Saturday Review*, reprinted in the *St. Louis University News*, Oct. 30, 1953.

14. *Ibid.*

15. John Stuart Mill, *On Liberty* . . . , p. 34.

16. Paul Hutchinson, *The New Ordeal of Christianity*, quoted in a book review by Father Edward Duff, S.J., in *Social Order*, June, 1957, p. 283.

17. Francis M. Rogers, quoted in *St. Louis Review*, Feb. 14, 1958.

18. *Ibid.*

19. *Dennis* v. *United States*, 341 U.S. 494, 584–85 (1951), dissenting opinion.

20. Rabbi Robert P. Jacobs, quoted in *St. Louis Post-Dispatch*, Jan. 16, 1954.

21. *Ibid.*

22. Samuel Eliot Morison, *Freedom in Contemporary Society* (Boston: Little, Brown and Company, 1956), pp. 106, 143.

23. *U.S.* v. *Schwimmer*, 279 U.S. 644, 654–55 (1929), dissenting opinion.

24. *U.S.* v. *Macintosh*, 283 U.S. 605, 633–34 (1931).

25. *Minersville School Dist.* v. *Gobitis*, 310 U.S. 586, 606–607 (1940), dissenting opinion.

26. Mr. Justice Douglas, "The Black Silence of Fear," *The New York Times Magazine*, January 13, 1952.

27. Ernest Barker, *Principles of Social and Political Theory*, pp. 268, 276.

28. Alfred North Whitehead, *Adventures of Ideas*, p. 69.

29. Barker, *op. cit.*, p. 277.

## Chapter XI (*pages 164–175*)

1. *The Needs of Higher Education in Maryland*. The Report of the Commission appointed by Governor Theodore R. McKeldin to Study the Needs of Higher Education in Maryland, 1955, p. 106.

2. *A Study of the Need for Additional Centers of Public Higher Education in California* (Sacramento: California State Department of Education, 1957), p. 101.

3. *Ibid.*, pp. 95–96.

4. *New York Times*, Jan. 20, 1957.

5. *Ibid.*

6. *Ibid.*

7. *Ibid.*

8. *Ibid.*, Jan. 25, 1957.

9. *A Study of the Need for Additional Centers of Public Higher Education in California*, p. 97.

10. *Ibid.*, p. 78.

11. Marquette University, Milwaukee, in 1957 completed a dormitory to accommodate 600 students in double rooms at construction costs of $4,712 per occupant, but the project cost per occupant reached $5,577. However, the university completed a dormitory in 1952 for 340 students at a project cost of $3,359 per occupant.

12. *School Life*, official journal of the Office of Education, U.S. Department of Health, Education, and Welfare, XXXX (Oct., 1957), p. 5.

13. *Ibid.*

14. It is of course virtually impossible to project the operating expenses to 1970. Too many variables are involved. In November, 1956, the Public Expenditure Survey of Wisconsin reported that annual operating costs in 72 city (public) systems in Wisconsin rose 8.3% in the last school year, from $300 to $317 per pupil. In Milwaukee there was an increase of $9.69 to $335.82 per pupil.

15. M. Clemens Johnson and C. George Lind, *Opening Enrollment in Higher Institutions, Fall, 1956*. Office of Education, U.S. Department of Health, Education, and Welfare, Jan. 1957, p. 7.

16. *Ibid.*, p. 12.

17. Simeon E. Leland, "The Problem of Numbers in Higher Education: From the Standpoint of Private Education," *College and University*, XXXI (Spring, 1956), p. 279.

18. Benjamin Fine, *New York Times*, Jan. 27, 1957.

19. *The President's Committee on Education Beyond the High School. Second Report to the President* (Washington: U.S. Government Printing Office, 1957), p. 6.

20. It is a reasonable assumption that tuition charges for resident students in state colleges and universities will not increase more rapidly than the operating costs per student. This thinking was reflected in the President's Committee on Education Beyond the High School recommendation (p. 23) "that charges to students in public institutions in general be increased no faster than the pace of family discretionary income. . . ."

## Chapter XII (*pages 176–204*)

1. *The Report of the Commission on Financing Higher Education: Nature and Needs of Higher Education* (New York: Columbia University Press, 1952), p. 31.

2. *Higher Education: Education Directory, 1956–1957*, Part 3. Office of Education, U.S. Department of Health, Education, and Welfare (Washington: U.S. Government Printing Office, 1956), p. 11.

3. *Statistics of Higher Education: Receipts, Expenditures and Property, 1953–54*, Chap. 4, Sec. II. Biennial Survey of Education in the United States—1952–54. Office of Education, U.S. Department of Health, Education, and Welfare (Washington: U.S. Government Printing Office, 1957), p. 8.

4. *Ibid.*, p. 32.

5. *Ibid.*, p. 44.

6. *Ibid.*, pp. 16–17.

7. *Ibid.*, p. 33.

8. *Ibid.*, pp. 17, 33.

9. *Ibid.*, pp. 74–78.

10. *Second Report to the President. The President's Committee on Education Beyond the High School* (Washington: U.S. Office of Education, 1957), p. 99.

11. *Ibid.*

12. *Ibid.*

13. *Ibid.*, p. 100.

14. *New York Times* (editorial), June 13, 1957.

15. *New York Times*, May 13, 1957.

16. *Ibid.*

17. *Ibid.*

18. *Ibid.*

19. *St. Louis Review*, Aug. 2, 1957.

20. *Ibid.*

21. *Ibid.* These small gifts are in sharp contrast to grants made to "big name" schools. The recent $15,000,000 gift to Yale University by the Old Dominion Foundation, established by Paul Mellon, reflects the gift-giving pattern of American foundations. The same foundation gave Yale $2,000,000 in 1949 and $5,000,000 in 1952 —a total of $22,000,000 in less than 10 years from a single foundation. *New York Times*, June 9, 1958.

22. *Statistics of Higher Education: Receipts, Expenditures and Property, 1953–54*, Chap. 4, Sec. II, p. 2.

23. *Ibid.*, p. 18.

24. *Ibid.*, pp. 3, 67.

25. *Ibid.*, pp. 8–9.
26. *Ibid.*, p. 68.
27. *Ibid.*, p. 9.
28. *Ibid.*, p. 33.
29. *Ibid.*, pp. 22–23.
30. *New York Times*, March 31, 1957.
31. *New York Times*, Feb. 26, 1958.
32. *New York Times*, Aug. 1, 1957, letter to the Editor.
33. John J. Theobald, "Higher Education for the Many," *College and University: The Journal of the American Association of Collegiate Registrars and Admissions Officers*, XXXI (Summer, 1956), 452.
34. Martin Quanbeck, "Implications of Increasing Enrollments for Academic Standards and Methods," *Educational Record*, XXXVIII (April, 1957), 127.
35. *Ibid.*
36. *Ibid.*, p. 127.
37. Simeon E. Leland, "The Problem of Numbers in Higher Education: From the Standpoint of Private Institutions," *College and University*, XXXI (Spring, 1956), 284.
38. *Ibid.*, p. 449.
39. *Ibid.*, p. 450.
40. *Ibid.*, p. 285.
41. *Statistics of Higher Education: Receipts, Expenditures and Property, 1953–54*, Chap. 4, Sec. II, p. 63.
42. *Ibid.*, p. 69.
43. R. H. Knapp and H. B. Goodrich, *Origins of American Scientists* (Chicago: The University of Chicago Press, 1952), p. 22.
44. *Ibid.*
45. *AIP Educational Newsletter*, published by the American Institute of Physics, April 15, 1958.
46. *Ibid.*
47. *Ibid.*
48. *New York Times*, Oct. 27, 1957.
49. *Teacher Supply and Demand in Colleges and Universities, 1955–56 and 1956–57*. A Study Conducted by the Research Division of the National Education Association, 1957, p. 32.
50. *Ibid.*

# Index

Academic freedom, 156, 159-160; threatened by the state, 51-52; defended by the Church, 52

Adams, John, 82

Alexander, Julian P., Justice, 54, 117, 119

American Alumni Council, 188

American Association of Land-Grant Colleges and State Universities, 20

American Bar Association, 27

*American Communications Assn.* v. *Douds*, 48-49

American Council on Education, 21

American Institute of Physics, 199, 200

Anderson, Robert Bernerd, 89-91

Association of American Colleges, 21

Baptist orphanages, support of children in, 207-208

*Barbier* v. *Connolly*, 112n.

Barker, Ernest, 3-5, 8, 10, 12, 15, 161-162

Beckman, Arnold L., 63-64

Bell, Bernard Iddings, 24, 47-48, 51-52, 63, 93, 98, 102-103, 104, 126, 130, 134

Benefits of education: moral and spiritual, 133-134; for democracy, 134; for struggle against tyranny, 135-136; preparation for citizenship, 137; business and professional, 137-138; cultural, 138; derived from all schools, 138-139; society should pay for, 139-142

Bestor, Arthur, 64-67, 148

Black, Hugo L., Justice, 48

Boggs, Hale, Congressman, 21

Boring, M. M., 62

Brain power: development of, 70-77; waste of, 71, 74; shortage of, 73-74

Brandeis, Louis D., Justice, 116-117

Bus transportation, 114-115

Butler, Nicholas Murray, 52

California Institute of Technology, 73

Case, Clifford P., Senator, 166

Catholic orphanages, support of children in, 207-208

Censorship: of selection, 86-87, 157-158, 215; by economic pressure, 158

Certificate or tax credit plan: meaning, 26-28; grants no aid to schools, 28-29; the education of veterans, war orphans, and page boys, 30

Challenge, intellectual, 65, 68, 70, 72, 76

*Chance* v. *Mississippi State Textbook Rating and Purchasing Board*, 55, 117-120

Choice in education: essential for freedom, 151-152; penalized, 151; and voluntary associations, 152; reduces the power of government, 153; and free discussion, 156-159

Church Federation of Greater Chicago, 104

Civil disabilities, 48

Classifications: and the law's purpose, 112-113, 115; of children and students, 112, 114-115; arbitrary and unreasonable, 113-115; based on thought and belief, 117-119

*Cochran* v. *Board of Education*, 31

Colonial colleges, philosophical and theological orientation of, 80-83

Commands, constitutional: to preserve freedom of mind and spirit, 57, 60

Commission on Financing Higher Education, 15, 176

Competition in education, 63-66; the challenge of, 144; consequences of lack of, 145-146; through direct subsidies, 146; eliminated by government monopoly, 145; advantages of, 145-146; and parental freedom of choice, 147; diversity,

225